"*The Night Window,* the new collaboration between Robert L. Dean, Jr. and Jason Baldinger brings the two artists together in a powerful, uncompromising collection of poetry and photography. Both Dean and Baldinger have repeatedly proven themselves as top-notch chroniclers of the human condition, and *The Night Window* seamlessly cements this status in grand fashion. Baldinger's photographs grab the eye, inviting the viewer to question all. The photography poses countless queries, offers no answers, but invites the viewer to dig deeper. And that is precisely where Dean comes in; documenting a world of "built-in obsolescence." A world where "the Lord's janitor/pulls the plug." A world where "Chill[s] caress upon the heart." All is laid bare in this ambitious and impressive collection as the two investigate the "Godzillas of the afterlife." Though much of the book unflinchingly reports on the less than glamorous side of americana, there is still plenty of room for hope. Indeed, Dean advises the reader. "the cavity inside the tire's flesh/is not entirely hollow." Ultimately, *The Night Window* is a powerful and necessary document that invites the reader to search for their own version of "the Futures we wanted."

-James Benger, author of *Floating Downstream*

"*The Night Window:* Ekphrastic poems and short fictions is a collection of writing and images exquisitely paired: each a finely crafted artistic statement standing alone yet each made greater and more expansive when brought together. Of course that is the essence of fine ekphrasis, the quality every artist seeks to achieve but often finds elusive. Baldinger has an eye for the arcane, the iconic everyday ordinariness of scenes that capture the battered soul of America's Rust Belt remnants, and he documents them, enshrines them, immortalizes them; they are images rich in narrative possibility, steeped in mystery, filled deep with untold tales. And Dean sees all these aspects in the photos: traces in words the weft and warp of their intricate tapestries, polishes the sheen of the faded dreams, lives, and loves of those who once dwelled in each picture's place, gives voice to the people who are invariably absent from view. The extraordinarily insightful poems and short prose crafted by Master of Ekphrasis Robert L. Dean, Jr. in response to the graphically stunning black and white photographs of Photographer/Documentarian Jason Baldinger are like facing mirrors; look into either and see the infinity of reflections each makes in the other, cascading as far as we readers/viewers can see, invoking unanticipated emotions, opening unexpected vistas, revealing unimagined worlds through *The Night Window.*"

-Roy Beckemeyer, author of *The Currency of His Light.*

"The poems in *The Night Window,* Robert L. Dean's latest collection, defy any notion that ekphrastic writing is merely simple exercise. He brings to Jason Baldinger's lush black & white images his entire body of life experience, weaves tales and recollections into a melancholy work that looks at, in, around, and beyond the photos presented. Dean's poems are intelligent, present, and offer a kind of equal companionship to the reader. As he says in, "Breath of the Lord," 'This is what I hear/ in the dooryard of my/ seventy-first year, approaching/ the tumble-down patchwork/ of what's to come.' We join in a three-way conversation with Dean and Baldinger, and come out all the more human for it."

-Cheryl Rice, author of *Love's Compass*

"This ekphrastic collection, *The Night Window* ties the visual and the written art together to cohabitate in harmony on the page. A picture is worth a thousand words. As I have aged, I have found some truth to that saying, but I have also found that I greatly enjoy the words. What's worth more? Hell, that's for you to decide for yourself, I am simply just telling you what I enjoy. Jason Baldinger's photographs show pieces of a life loved, lost, abandoned and forgotten…reflected into and juxtaposed with the slow but still present heartbeat of this beautiful disaster of a world we navigate. Robert L. Dean, Jr.'s writing is the pacemaker to Baldinger's photographs. His words generate pulses and are skillfully crafted to tell the stories of the loved, lost, abandoned and forgotten before the beautiful disaster turns everything to darkness… and at that point, it's too damn late."

- Victor Clevenger, author of *Every Angel in Heaven
is a Hopscotch Champion*

THE NIGHT WINDOW

Ekphrastic poems and short fictions

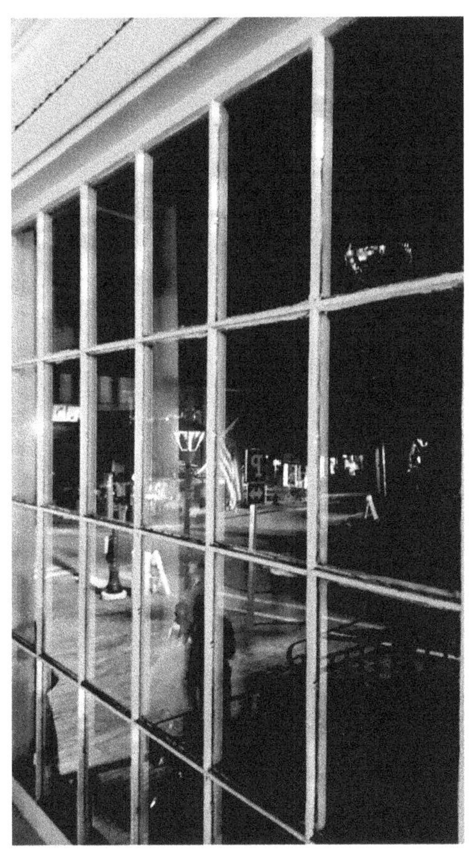

Texts by Robert L. Dean, Jr

Photographs by Jason Baldinger

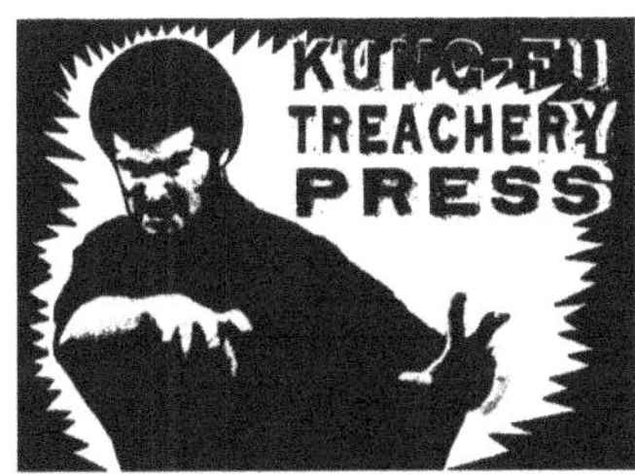

Kung Fu Treachery Press,

Rancho Cucamonga, California

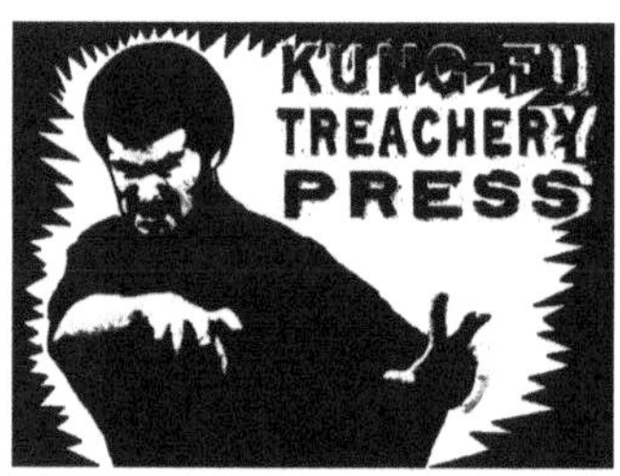

Acknowledgements

The authors gratefully acknowledge the editors and staff of the following publications, in which these collaborations first appeared:

MacQueen's Quinterly: "A Well-Lighted Place;" "Breath of the Lord;" "Old Style;" "Subject To;" "Temporarily Condemed;" "Window Dressing."

Synkroniciti: "A Blossom Fell;" "BOLO;" "Cat People;" "Dead Man's Hollow;" "Look Up."

The Ekphrastic Review: "Airstream;" "Cloister;" "Escape;" "Full Immersion;" "Heaven From Here;" "Home Town Girl;" "Judgement Day;" "Luna Pier;" "Modern and Other -isms;" "Smile You Are;" "Standard Time;" "Stop;" "The Hang Up;" "The Night Window;" "Twister."

The author and the photographer would like to thank Jason Ryberg of Osage Arts Community for his commitment in shaping this book.

Table of Contents

In 2016, I set off on a reading tour with my buddy, and fellow poet Scott Silsbe. We did a few bad shows and got a set of even better stories out of the first few dates. We had to make one of those deadly all-day drives from Chicago to Kansas City before then heading to Lawrence, Kansas for a reading at The Raven. I was so bloody tired that all I have are snippets, still frame photographs of that night. The next night we would read in Blue Springs, MO and I would meet another flock of wayward poets who would become friends, drinking buddies, agitators, and collaborators. It seems strange looking back almost ten years, how much magic would derive from a few brief encounters half a country away.

Bob got in touch fall of 2022, when we were all a little windblown and he requested I send over photos he'd seen on facebook. After the first few poems our rapport grew, so when I was out shooting, and a shot would spark Bob's poems, I'd reach out to him. A couple years have passed and we arrive at *The Night Window*. In rereading this book again, I'm in awe of the of the depth these words add to the images I've collected. These moments of American Loneliness and American Mortality and whatever else can be said of Americana become at once, even larger with the addition of these poems. Bob found the voice is those shots, in those reflections, across those lonely streets and in the eye of every mannequin. His voice amplifies what he's seeing and a fusion, a simple grace is achieved there. That moment where two artforms at their best meet, that is true collaboration. Thanks Bob.

-Jason Baldinger

To the best of my recollection, I first met Jason Baldinger at The Raven Bookstore in Lawrence, Kansas, in 2016, at which Jason was a feature reader, as was my friend Roy Beckemeyer, with whom I tagged along. Somewhere along the line, I discovered Jason's photographs on Jason's Face Book page and bugged Jason to let me write to some. Jason capitulated. The first of the collaborations was "Heaven From Here" in November of 2022, followed immediately by "The Hangup," both of which appeared in *The Ekphrastic Review* on December 3, 2022. A total of 26 works, consisting of poems, flash fictions, and hybrids, appeared over the next two years, all of which were fortunate enough to receive publication in various ekphrastic journals. For me, it has been a joy to write to Jason's wonderful, often quirky, photographs. I should make it clear that all of Jason's photographs existed in their own right before I wrote to them. We have been fortunate to have terrific publishers in Lorette C. Luzajic at *The Ekphrastic Review,* Clare MaQueen at *MacQueen's Quinterly,* and Katharine Grace McDaniel at *Synkroniciti.* We hope you find something that moves you in this collection of words and images.

Robert L. Dean, Jr.

And when I say you are dreaming, I am dreaming too.

-Zhuangzi

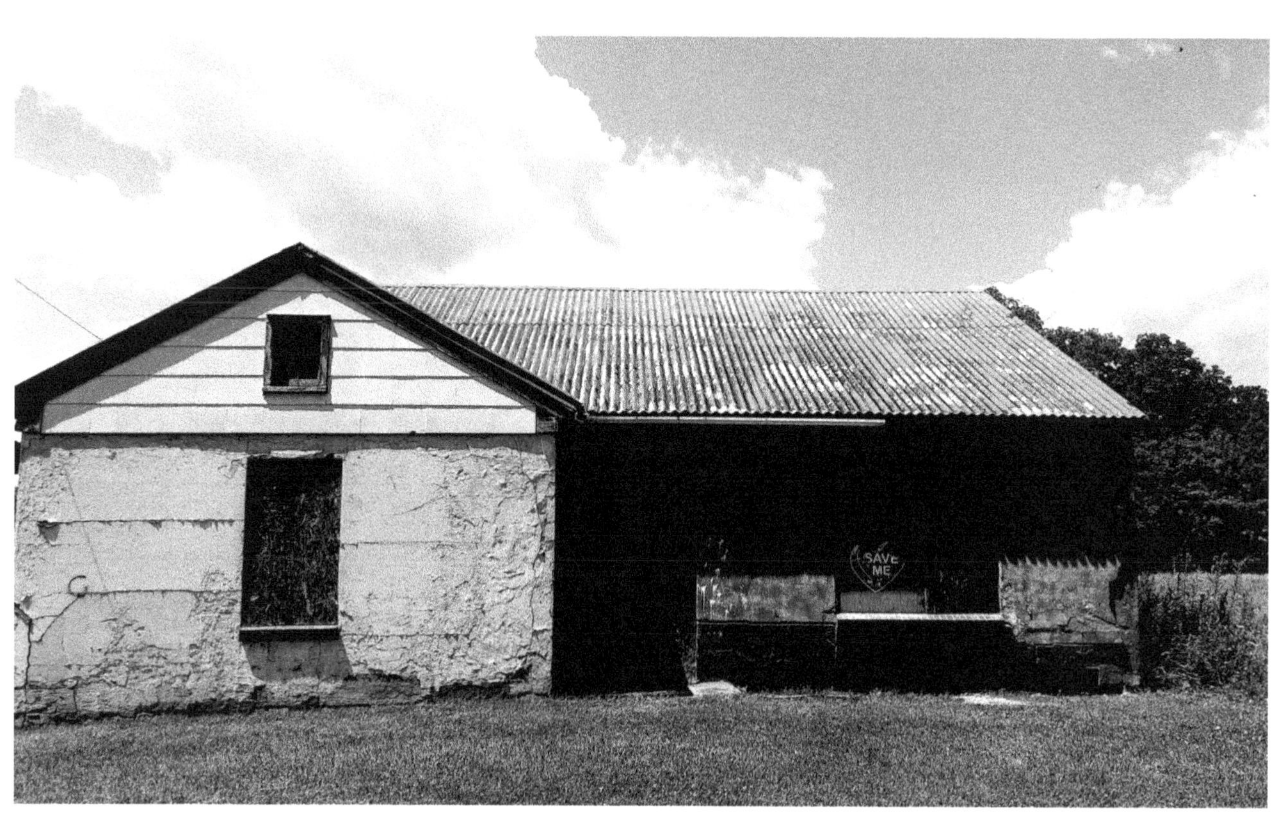
SAVE
ME

Breath of the Lord

Whisper strokes
the beard of earth,

rolls in
on clouded chariots,

stutters through
the break of trees,
neglect of weeds,

a sotto voce
of times past,
lives moved on,

the arterial bypass
of freeways from

one congested heart
to another,

the lowered pulse
of voided humanity,

the spaces we left
behind, the endangered species
of memory.

This is what I hear
in the dooryard of my

seventy-first year, approaching
the tumble-down patchwork
of what's to come,

calling out halloos
to the shadowed door-mouth,
blinded eye-windows,

at last recognizing
the "Save Me" handiwork
emblazoned under the eave,

the scrawl that made me
stop and get out of the car,

realize at just the moment I knock
that this is the place
from which I embarked.

No longer does a voice cry out
in the wilderness. I have prepared
the way, and when the door opens,

I flicker like candle's breath
across the face of the waters.

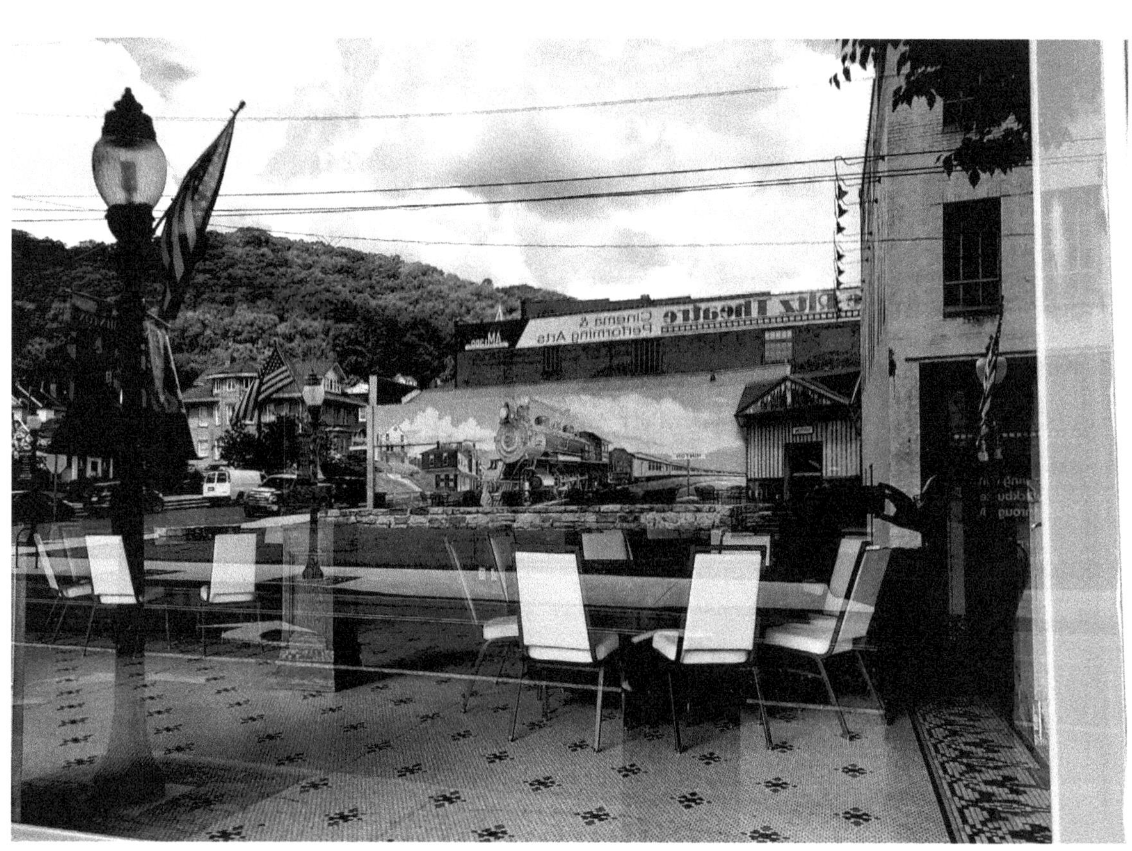

Heaven From Here

The train arrives, or, not quite, really,
still belching, no squeal of iron on iron,
no one there to hear it, platform empty,

the sign of who we are backwards, perhaps
we have been or will be or are passed by,
history on display at the Ritz, an audience of

ghost chairs, stacking metal and vinyl banquet
on mosaic Depression tile, floral pattern
long wilted, like us, are we in or out,

we can't make up our minds, maybe we'll turn
left, maybe right, one arrow pointing us
toward the train, the other in the direction

it is headed, or was headed, or we remember it
being headed, or would remember, if we were still
here, still performing, still listening for the whistle

of time rolling in, the drum-drum heartbeat of
shako-plumed youth celebrating whatever it is
we used to celebrate, lamp-post flags waving

once again in the breeze that is surely locomoting in
on the dark underbelly of sky, one lone tourist
trying to capture us, ghost that he is and always will be.

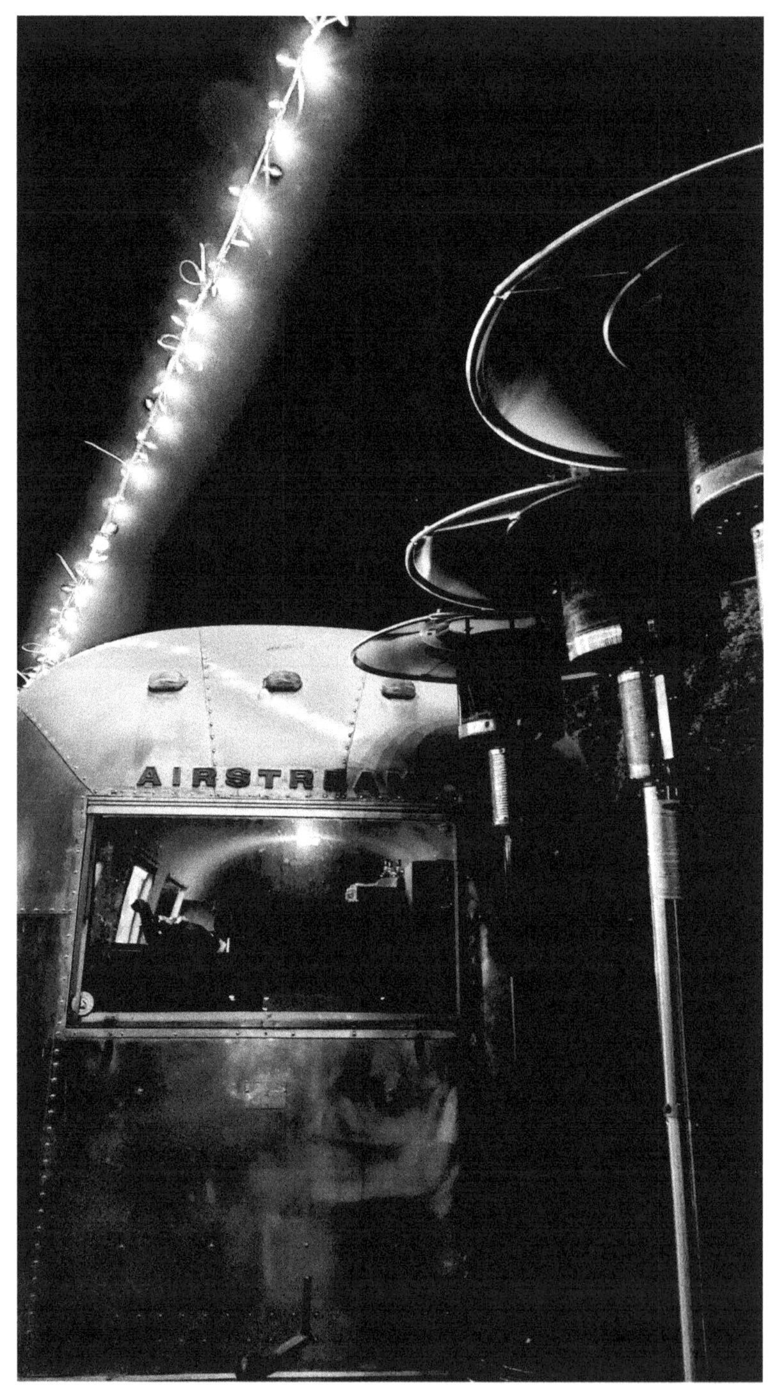
AIRSTREAM

Airstream

Amazing. Astounding.
Buck Rogers. The Jetsons.
The Future now playing
in the rear view,

all shiny and metallic,
tailgated by aliens,
friendly or hostile
depending on one's point of view.

Still UFO but now
stanchioned into memory,

crowd control pretenders
preparing for ghostly queues
of kids with ray-guns, phasers, lightsabers.

Three day work weeks, work from home,
robotic houses, cars that read your mind.
These were the Futures we wanted.

Doublethink, the ignition point
of books, HAL, androids dreaming
of electric sheep—informational,
apocalyptic, romantic, maybe,

but these were
the Futures
that scared us.

AI we say,
now that it's here,
and shrug.

There is nothing wrong
with your television set.

Maybe I wrote this,
maybe I phoned it in,
flipped a switch,
maybe I'm cruising

the air streams,
pouring a whiskey
from the wet bar,
lighting the AI fireplace,

stars strung overhead,
taking those little green men
---who, in the end,
only wanted to warn us---

to the Outer Limits.
We repeat: There is nothing wrong

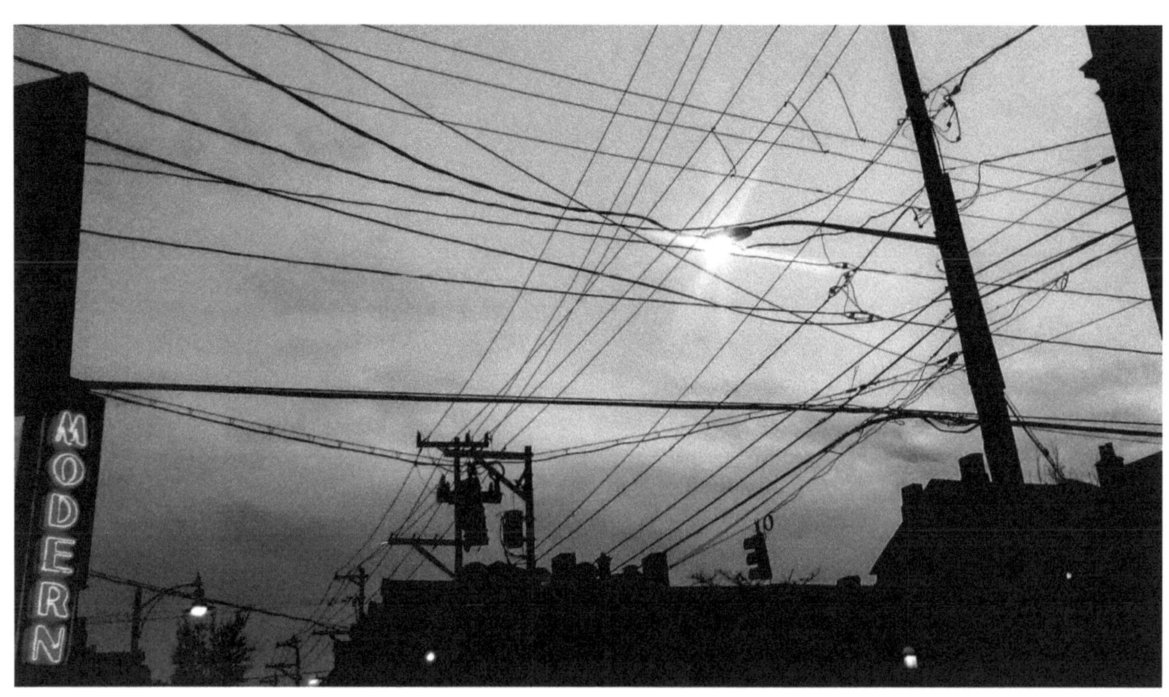

MODERN

Modern, and Other -isms

But is it? Can it truly be, modern? Or are we
postmodern here, looking back on what we once
thought of as modern? Aren't we in the instant that is after
the instant that was now an instant ago? And wasn't this
modern postmodern to the modern that came before it?

Is this the place we stayed at last time? Or the deconstruction
we will be checking into once we park the rental? Perhaps it is staid,
sedate, the principled break we need; perhaps the experiential
scatology we've been looking forward to. It is forward, right? But
if it's post, aren't we backward? What if there are no crystal balls,

and the post-past is just a dream? I tell you the light above
is the sun in an overcast sky, you insist
it's a streetlight coming on at dusk. On second glance,
I concur with you. On retrospection,
you prefer my first impression.

All Cretans are liars, you say, trusting I remember Epimenides,
and the place of his birth. Or will, at any given moment.

Given. Is that how time works? Given, at any moment? If so,
by whom? Do we evolve, or are we creation ongoing? What if
we are both? Here tomorrow, gone today? The Ghetto Singers

in Theresienstadt play *Someday My Prince Will Come*
before the train for Auschwitz rolls in. McCartney sings of *Yesterday,*
Harrison of *Something.* Here, in the postmodern, you can feel the
neon pulse in red, hear the groan of green in the stoplight womb.
See the golden glow beyond the pale/pole, just the one, come on in the

second floor window—or is it the third? We can't visualize, after all, street
level, where structure begins. Someone up late. Or early? Don't let those
wires, those overhead threads, that Spider-Time's spun web, hang you up.
GPS is useless here. What you have is all you have. Where you have been
is who you are going is when you were. Arrival, departure, the same way station.

Keep it new, says Pound, in his pre-post-modern world. *Not under this sun,*
replies the prophet, three million moments before. And suddenly, nothing changes.

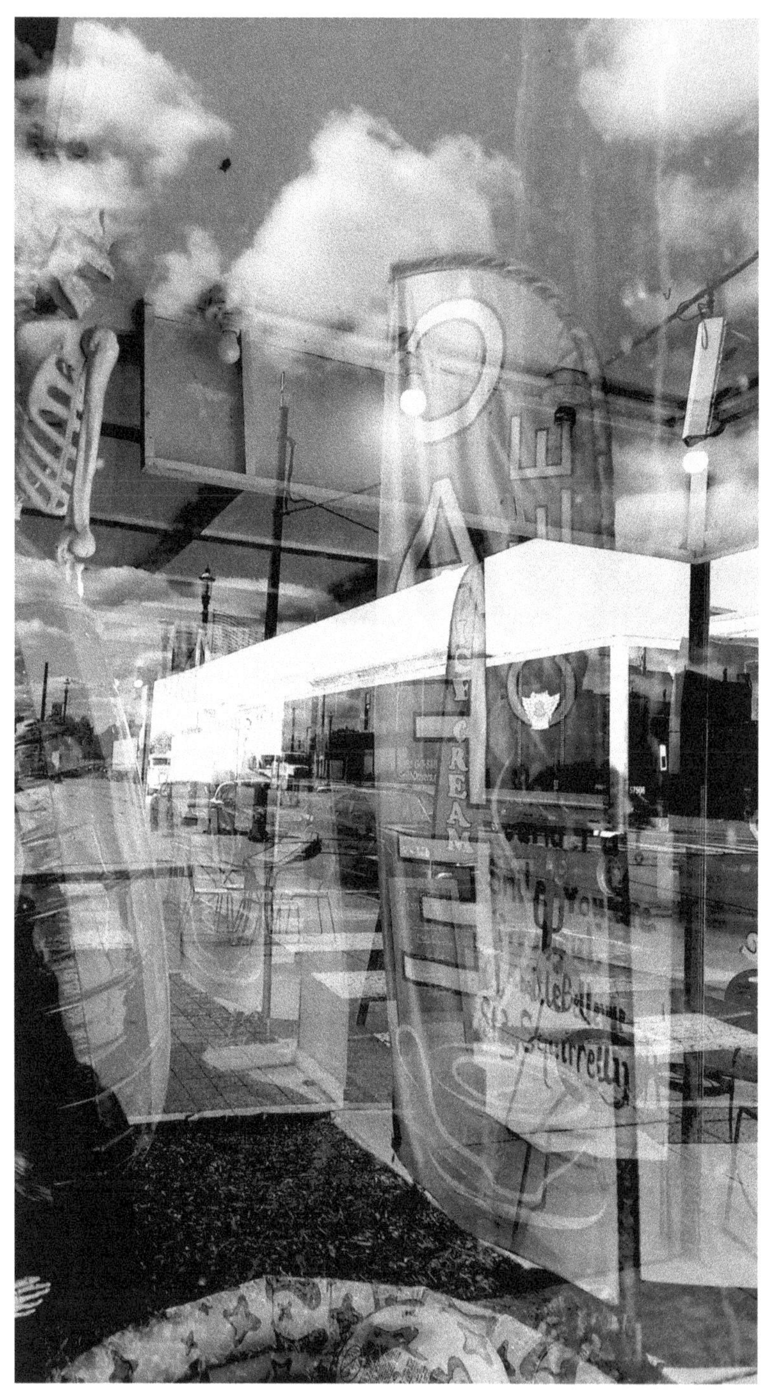

Smile You Are

Slack-jawed, sans flesh, sans all sense of
               who we were, we recycle from the chrysalis
of questions, of waiting to become, head in the clouds,
                  the last bulb of clarity yet to click on.

Drawn to what looks like stuck-on-a-pole redemption, in some other
              neighborhood, dimension, in the adulthood where we seem to recall
                  we used to live,
Godzillas of the afterlife, we lurch on, screeching like bad brakes towards the
                Promised Land Buffet,

loading up our piggy-back platters with Smith Transport, which transports us
              nowhere, fills nothing in the hold beneath our ribs,
                and we remain parked and hungry in front of
what may have been our lives, no longer rolling stock, with only the promise of
              ice cream and Edelweiss.

Echoes cackle, a subtraction of voices in the hollow high meadows of our skulls
              where memories are bone white and brief,
                like lives maybe,
like all the maybe lives we will ever live, have lived, will never live, like
              the one stubborn light which never enlightens.

Foot-bones stub against the inflatable pool of childhood
              with all its warnings,
          all its ignored hazards.
We settle in to shallowness, the place we once were happy,
            splash ourselves with the not yet learned and, like the sign says,
              stay squirelly.

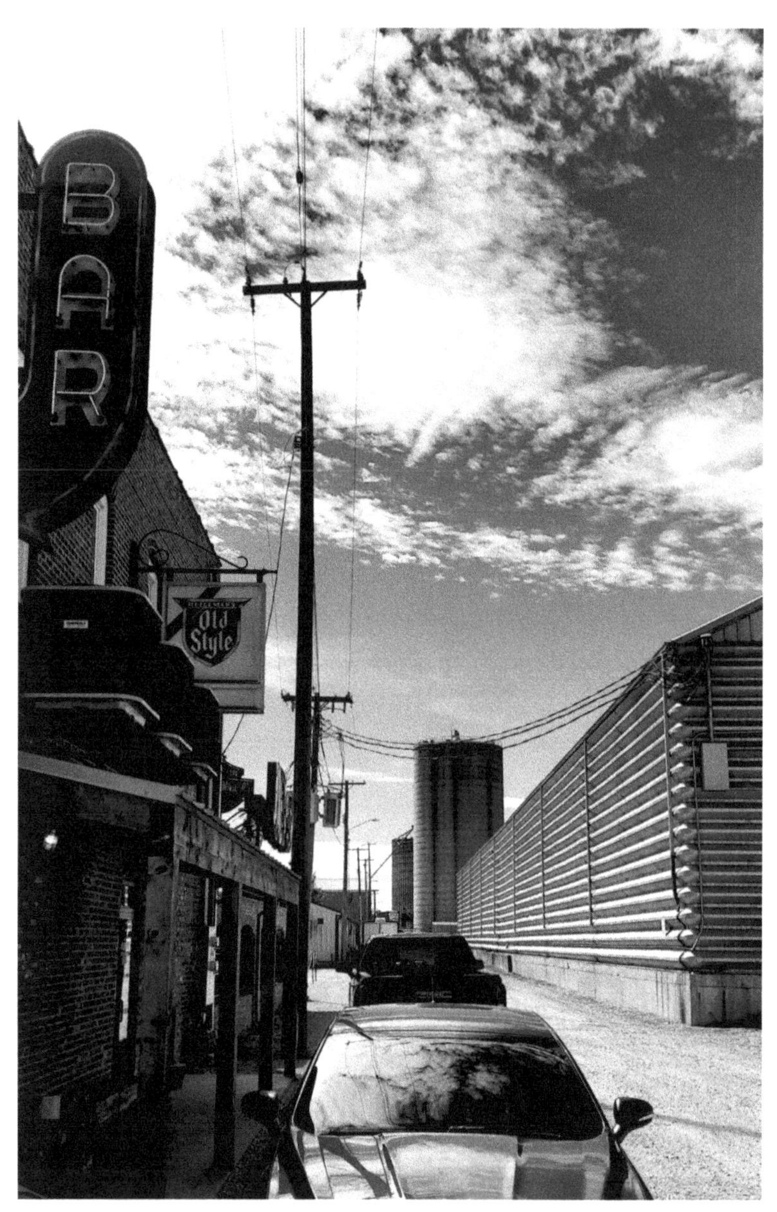

B
A
R
Old
Style

Old Style

This is the place where Slim overlooked the peeling corner of your fake ID and poured you a cold one because you were from the neighborhood and Slim's brother worked with your dad at the ball-bearing factory and Tiny Spinetti's neorealist cards were accepted currency all over town. This is the place with the best beef jerky and Cracker Jacks in the county and where Madge's pink skirt hiked up to mid-thigh when she wiped down the high stool tables. This is the place out back of which you and Albert Gutzmann got into your one and only fight, the place where legend says John Dillinger and Pretty Boy Floyd used to hang out between bank robberies. This is the place where guys in VFW jackets left their Harleys unchained and re-fought Incheon, Heartbreak Ridge, and a hill called Pork Chop, while a few college boys home on break debated the location of a place called Vietnam, and old men in John Deere and AFL-CIO caps puffed Luckies, Winstons, and Camels, the air above them a skeptical haze of Khrushchev, Cuba, and Berlin. Flippers and kickers pinged and dinged from one wall, steel points thunked cork on another, the crack of a nine-ball break came from a side room, money rustled from hand to hand. Mysterious metal ribs across the street kept watch, holding their breath, poker-chip towers marching into the vanishing point of history. The GMC out front is not the jalopy you remember, souped up by Crazy Eddie Nitschke, and you wonder, if you walk through the door right now, with your chip-embedded plastic license and wi-fi ear buds, if you can still get an Old Style in a frosted mug, if Slim still remembers, if the air is still drunk with glory.

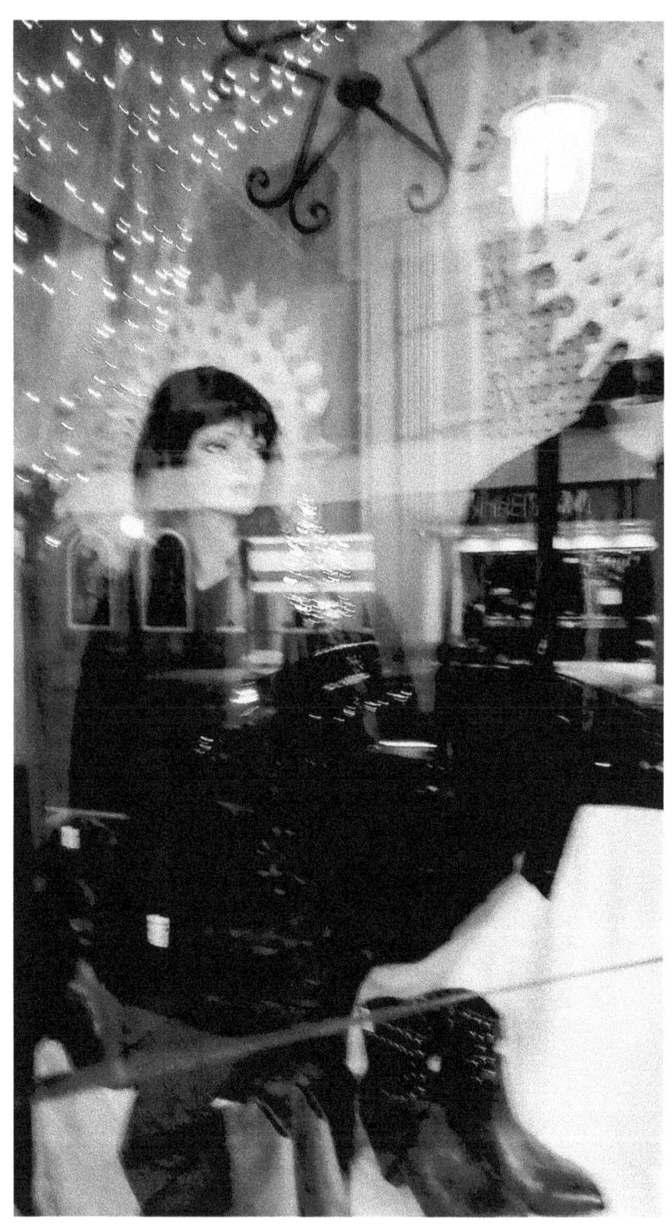

Home Town Girl

Sovereign of homecoming, prom, Founder's Day, Harvest Festival, her
crown is perhaps less dazzling these days, though reflective still of the *Ice
Queen* diadem some spurned tuba player gave her. Unapproachable, yes,
she could be. She had a plan, and attachment to this burg wasn't part of it.
Women's lib, she was all for it, if it meant liberation from here. But when the
Feminists marched down Main, she was getting a new doo at Betsy's Hair
and Nail Emporium. A photo shoot at Verne's would get her out. Verne
knew big people in big places, his pics had been in the Gazette, PennySaver,
once even National Enquirer. Flash bulbs flashed, shutters clicked, the phone
rang late at night, breathing, just breathing. Men looked at her differently on
the street. The preacher preached a sermon that did everything but mention
her name. She shelled out $500 for the negatives and Verne caught the
bus for L.A. Dior knock-offs in the epochs and eras that followed shed no
hometown dust. Grunge, goth, and saggy were brief aberrations. A veil
fluttered white, an organ played, an asteroid fell. And then, on a surprisingly
clear and sudden day, she looked around like she imagined the dinosaurs did
and found herself extinct. In this diorama, you can see her eyes enraptured
with that dreamy look. Expectation kisses her so life-like lips. On the other
side of the mirror, an elegant Rotary Club carriage awaits. I don't presume to
know if she is happy here, twinkling in the heaven of home town lore, but
she has that glow, just as she did in those high-flying moments right before
each regal wave.

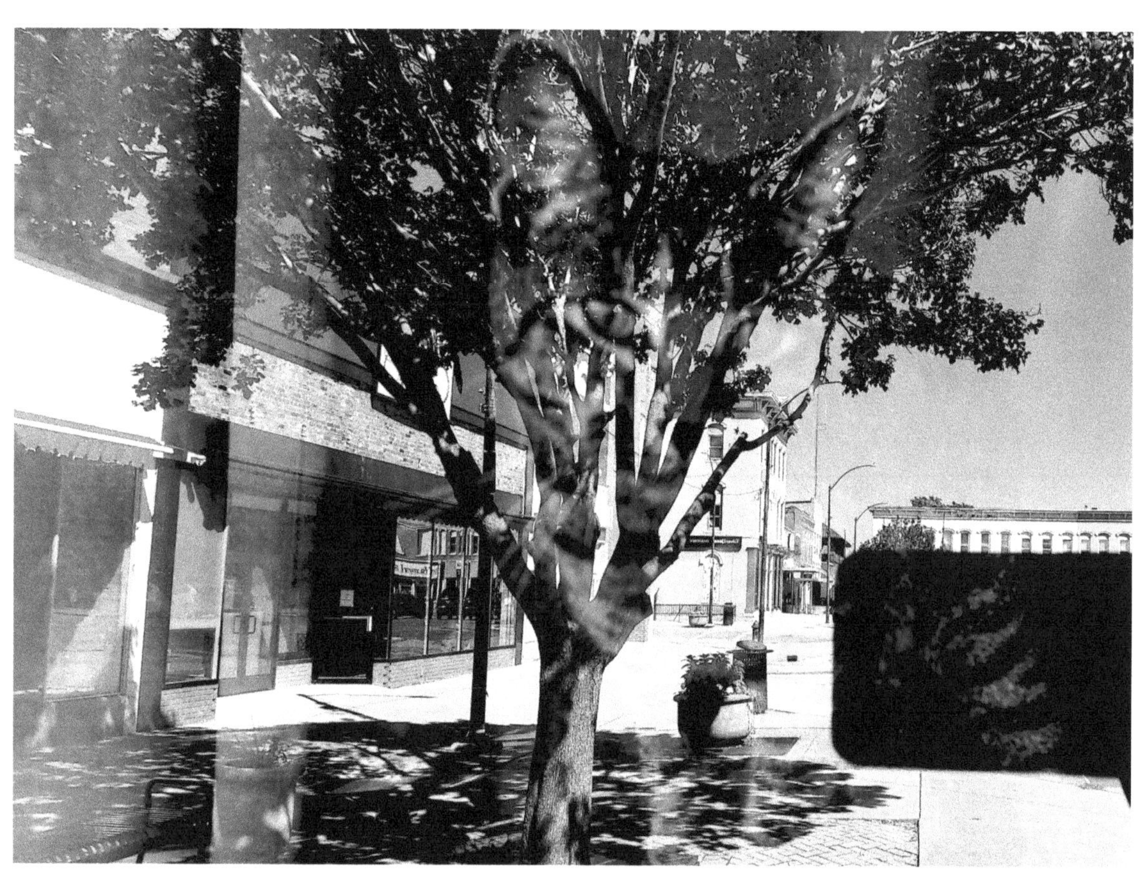

Cat People

No mere mousers, we. We loom up from trees, clear blue skies, the main streets of life, a feline aura at the edge of the subconscious. We are gamesters, pranksters. We toy and trifle, bat and paw, not to kill, but simply for sport. And when the plaything is played out, we bring it, tail between teeth, drop its lifeless body at your feet, sit back on our haunches and wait for a rub between the eyes, behind the ears, wherever our sweet spot is. We do not understand when you recoil. Isn't this, after all, what you wanted? A cellar free of rats?

We do not understand when you identify, momentarily at least, with the mangled. Why you are terrorized by the daggered points of our eyes, the narrowed depths of our black pupils. Your confusion over whose altar upon which we lay our sacrifice. The tight curl of our tails around our haunches, our neatly placed front paws. Our innate, audacious, catness.

Be not mistaken, however. We see you. Your dealings with your own kind. When you "civilized" us, what did you expect we'd learn? Nature versus nurture, you like to say, not truly understanding the difference. Not truly understanding what it is that haunts you.

And so you turn away from this reflection, seek out a dark alley, tail slinked between legs. A kitten hisses as you pass. You slaughter, and slaughter, and slaughter. Heedless, the sun arises.

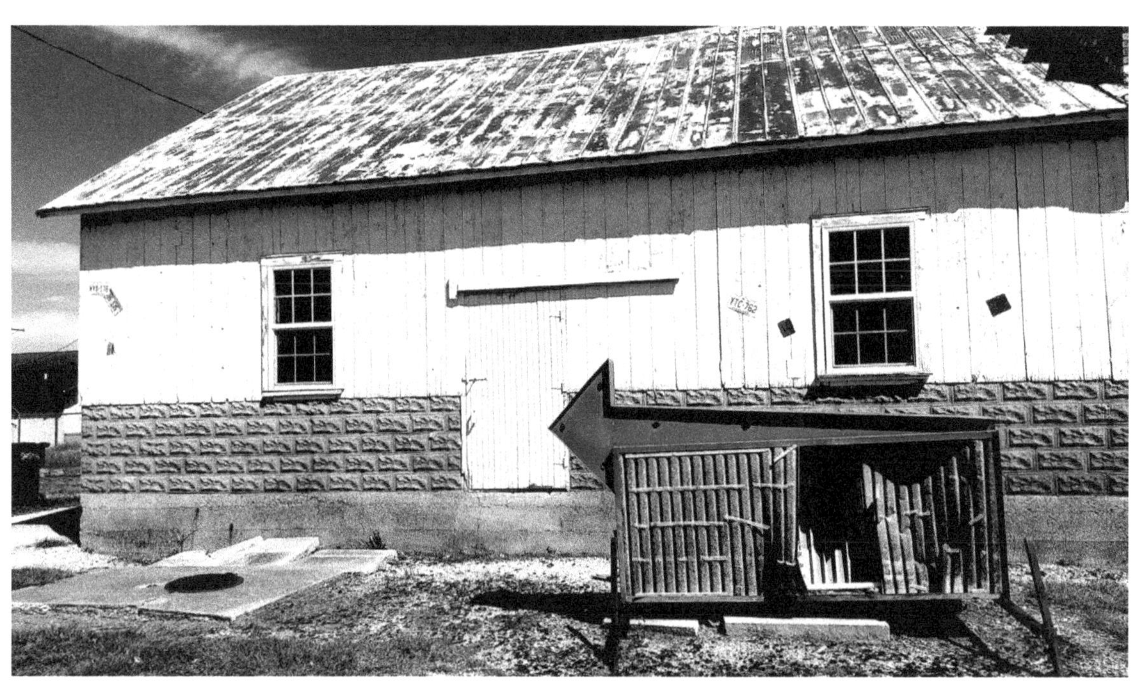

BOLO

What we know:
1: It is no longer among us (see hole in container).
2: It went that-away (see big arrow pointing left).
3: It is very powerful (see metal punched open from inside).
4: At least three vehicles were not involved in the escape (see license tags nailed to barn).
5: It did not go down the manhole (we looked).

What we do not know:
1: What it is wearing (if anything).
2: What alias it may be traveling under (we booked it as a John Doe—and yes, we looked).
3: If it's armed, though we know it's dangerous (see #3 "What we know" above, and
    our gut instinct).
4: When, exactly, it escaped, though we presume in the wee hours (we may have
    seen something of it in our nightmares).
5: What, exactly, it is (even though we looked).
6: Why there is a manhole on this farmstead (or a cage with an arrow on top, for
    that matter).

For purposes of this BOLO, we have assigned "it" code name FEAR. If you live
in this vicinity, lock your doors, bolt your windows. Do not traffic with strangers.
Report your suspicions to the authorities. We will take "it" from there, though two
deputies did not report in today and Orville is hitting the bottle again. Rest assured Big
Brother is watching (Wilbur was catching some ZZZs when this happened; Wilbur has
been disposed of, see "manhole" above) and we always get our man (or "it," or whatever).

We repeat, there is no need to panic. Even though we are:
1: Understaffed.
2: Outgunned.
3: Like Alice, down the rabbit hole (aka manhole, see above, though why she was
    down there, Alice didn't say, even at ten feet tall, like Grace Slick said she would).

   We will take no questions on fire, famine, plague or pestilence during this briefing. No
questions on lying in made beds. FEAR is the issue here, and the only thing we have to fear
is….well, you guessed it.

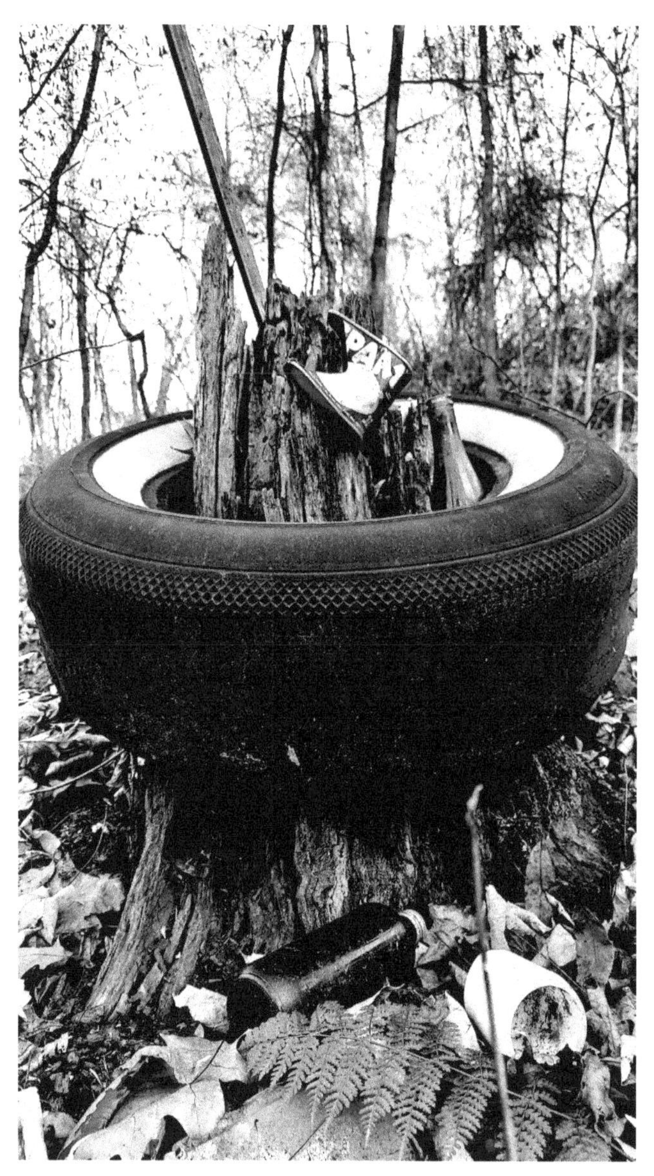

Dead Man's Hollow

It's not like they say.
I could have taken it with me.
I wanted to leave something
behind, a monument.
I suppose I could have chosen wiser.

I could, for example,
have chosen to leave
kindness, light, love.

Not the old lady crossing the street
kind of thing, but I could have given a damn
about somebody, somewhere.

You, for instance.
I could have cared
about you. I could have said:
*Please, Thank you, Hi
how are you?* Smiled
once in a while.
Laughed.
Cried.

Fed you when you were
hungry, clothed you
when you were naked.
Thrown my arms around you
when you needed me the most.

I could have chosen peace.

Instead, I carted around
all this rubbish,
day by day,

street by street,
continent to continent,
mistaking it for intimacy,
benevolence, compassion.

Don't get me wrong,
I did love you,
do love you,
will always love you,
though I wanted it
duty-free, no strings
attached, no debts incurred.

And so, I leave you this,
in remembrance of me.
Whatever your initial impression,
the cavity inside the tire's flesh
is not entirely hollow.
Lighter fluid and matches
slumber beneath the rim.
What use you put them to,
should you decide to awaken them,
is entirely up to you.

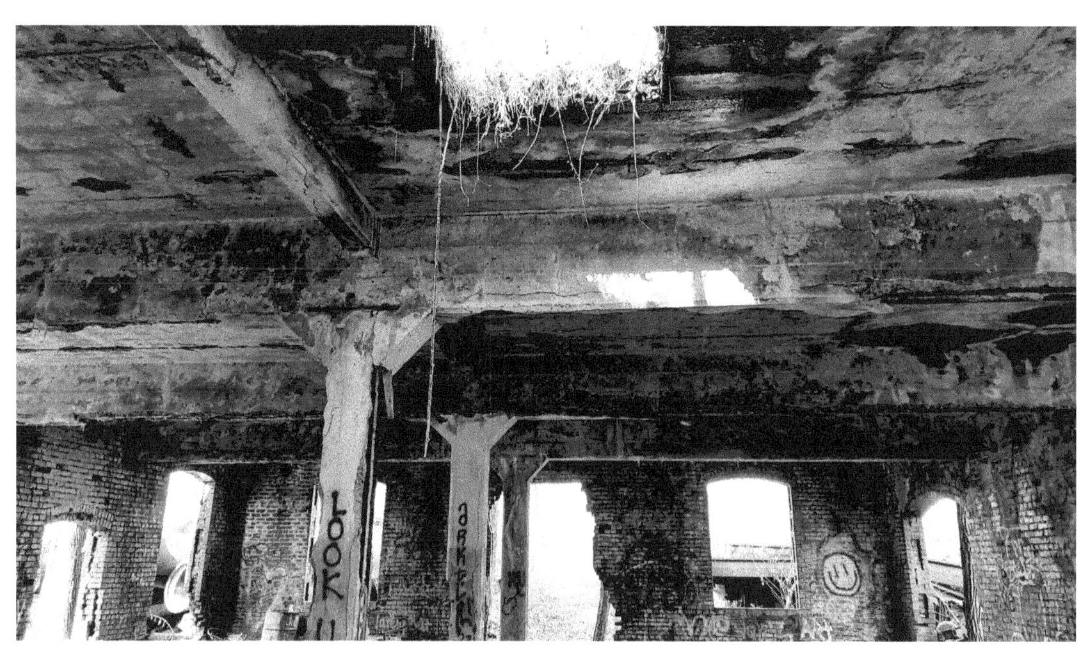

LOOK

Look Up

No Chicken Little parable here.
The sky is not falling. Light

flows in from all angles, the bright present
above, the misty past beyond.

It is actually the roof which has fallen---
or is it? The missing piece being, in fact,

a square, with precise edges,
maybe even some molding to shore open
the space. The grass

lets its hair down, like the scalp-covering
of one of those old-time prairie sod houses
with the dust-blackened family blowing
in treeless wind, only

no one lives here, has ever lived here. Those rough-shod
bricks, double-arched doors, cement butterfly pillars,

there was industry here once,
something built, mined, refined,

metal crying out under hammer blows,
2x4s shedding sawdust tears---
something, maybe,

a lift, harness, conveyor belt humming
in through the ceiling. What is that
viaduct, tramway, causeway that ends so

abruptly but hiddenly? What was it used for?
And that toilet basin or gold panning tub
gleaming, mouth wide open, in the sun to our left?

Was there treasure here? Is there treasure here still?
Is it possible? If not, then why is

the wall smiling
and why is that

little helmeted space man
peering in from the lower corner right?

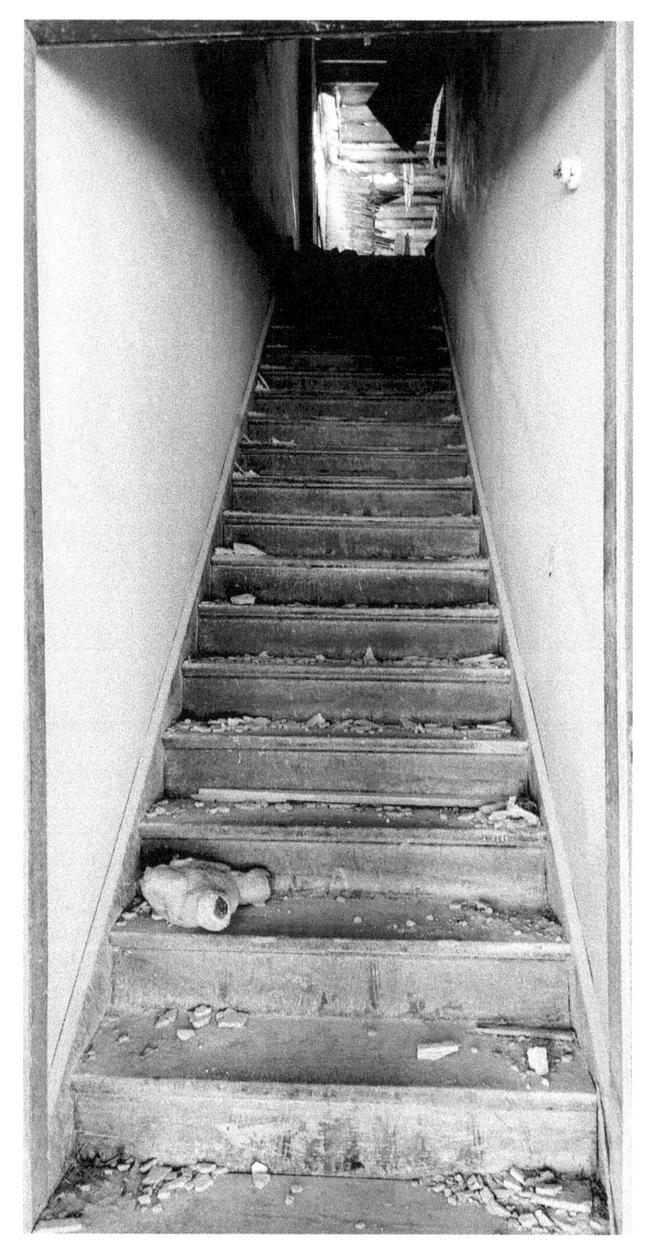

A Well-Lighted Place

We glance around for Orpheus, St. Peter, wonder if we are ascending to or descending from, find both lacking. Our own recognizance, then, in the midst of our own shambles. Heaven, it seems, is not as advertised. Hell, if that's what our backs are against, is country undiscovered, and we shudder at the thought of vistas more desolate than the present. Is the passage as it closes in littered with the debris of mortality, or eternity collapsing? We brace hands against walls, try to forestall what narrows. Have we lived in vain, are we dying for nothing? The dismembered thing on the step: something we dropped? A burden yet to carry? A life incomplete? What does the eye bulging from the sheet rock know? The glow at the top beckons, though shadow prefigures. Darkness as threshold to light. Magnetosphere in flux. Us, waiting for us. A compass jams. Water shatters. We tuck head against chest, draw in arms and legs. With a push of our own making, we expel from zygote way station into sagging gape of life and death, cleaving doubt as we go.

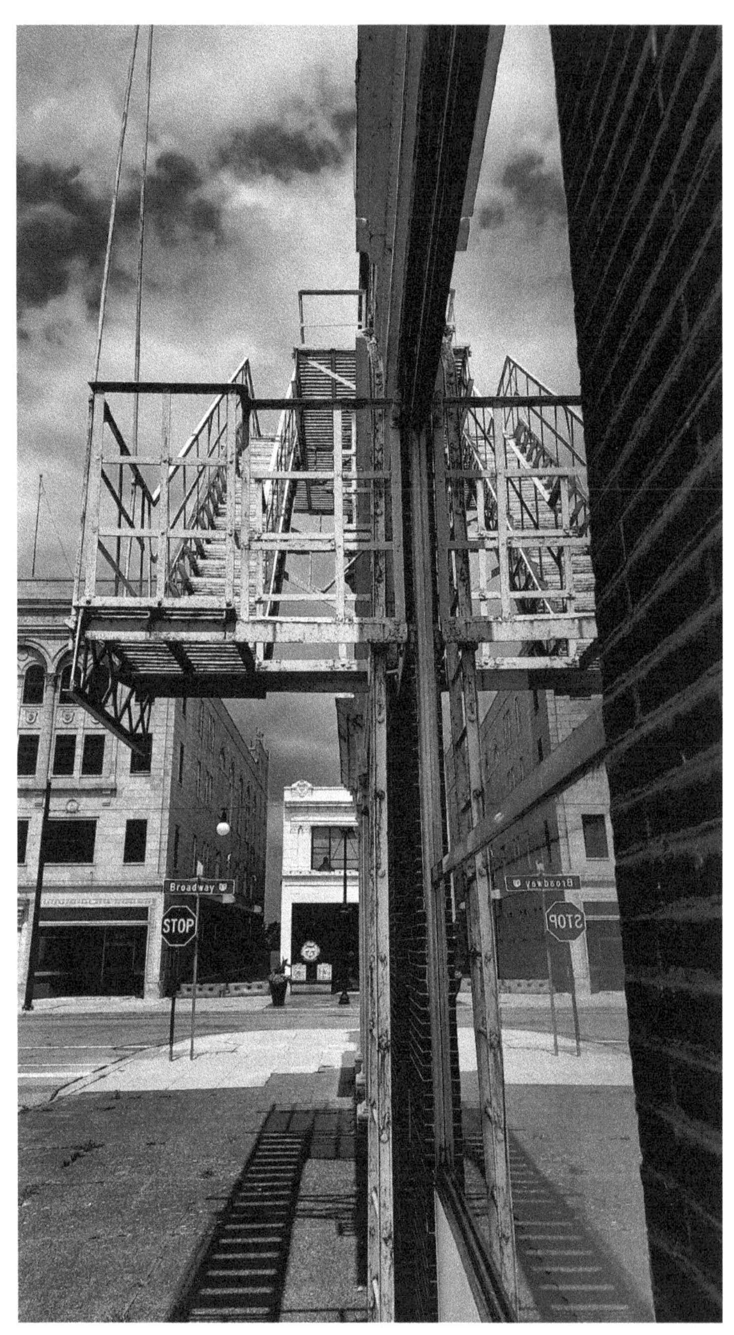

Escape

What sort of blueprint gave us this redundant stairway to nowhere? And why do we so blindly worship it? Surely such a sky was foreseen, such celestial conjuring forecast long ago. Not even a crossroads marks us, merely a T-bone. Had we intended to reach for the heavens? In a moment, the heavens will reach for us. The stop sign is facing the wrong way. We cannot help that we have given such a grandiose name to such a narrow lane in a no-stoplight town, it is in our nature. We are dreamers, schemers, stargazers. We reach for the impossible, improbable, unattainable, not expecting the dark to come for us one day, out of the blue, that we will need a way to get down as well as up, that we have cut ourselves off at the knees, drawn up no plans for retreat, no shelter from the storm. Perhaps if we take a right turn, follow that supernumerary Broadway into the reflection of our handiwork, we'll find a loophole in our intentions, a way out of our built-in obsolescence, an escape from the threat of the idols of us.

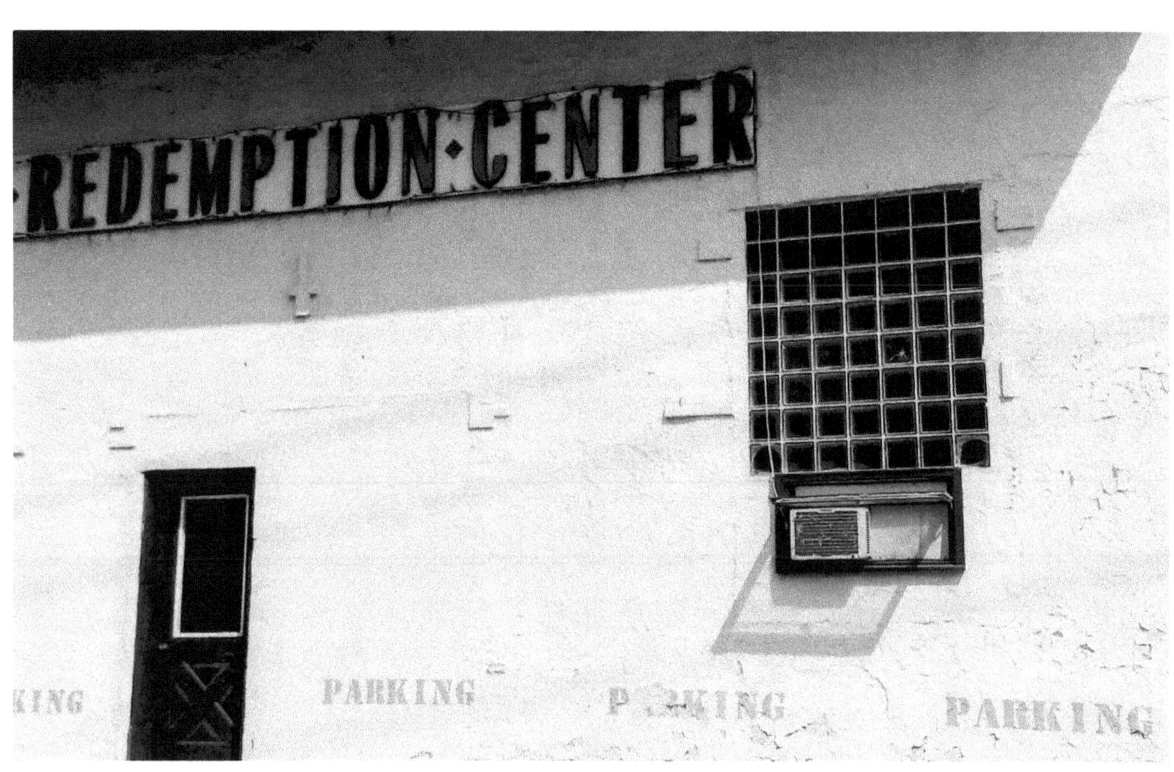
REDEMPTION·CENTER
KING
PARKING
P RKING
PARKING

Full Immersion

I seek the full immersion experience,
thumb and forefinger of holiness
clamping my nostrils, rainbowing me over,
other hand bracing the small of my back.

Around my hips the postulant's robe floats,
a white lily upon the face of the waters,
the preacher's salving words gurgling in and out
of my ear canals with the ebb and flow

of blue-green water, ceramic-tiled tub standing in
for the River Jordan. My sins wash away
with stains gone before, swirl down
the drain hole of redemption when the Lord's janitor

pulls the plug. I am pumped for sainthood,
pumped to be, at last, among the chosen,
to get my ass up off the sidelines, out of the bleachers,
rah-rah-sis-boom-bah the angelic band down the court
of Beulah-land to victory, the celestial spree
of slam dunks, buzzer-beaters, carried aloft
on winged shoulders of apostolic teammates.

I'm weary of rummaging mortal garbage pails
for heaven's leavings, holding cardboard signs
with sketchy pleas, kneading canned heat
into iced hands under crumbling bridges
from nowhere to nowhere. I'm tired

of the everyday, the 9-5, the humdrum, the absence
of wings ascending. The void of cars in the lot,
broken windows, lack of any wheeze from the A/C,
does not deter me. Christmas lights, after all, are up.
I am ready. Sweet Jesus, I am ready.

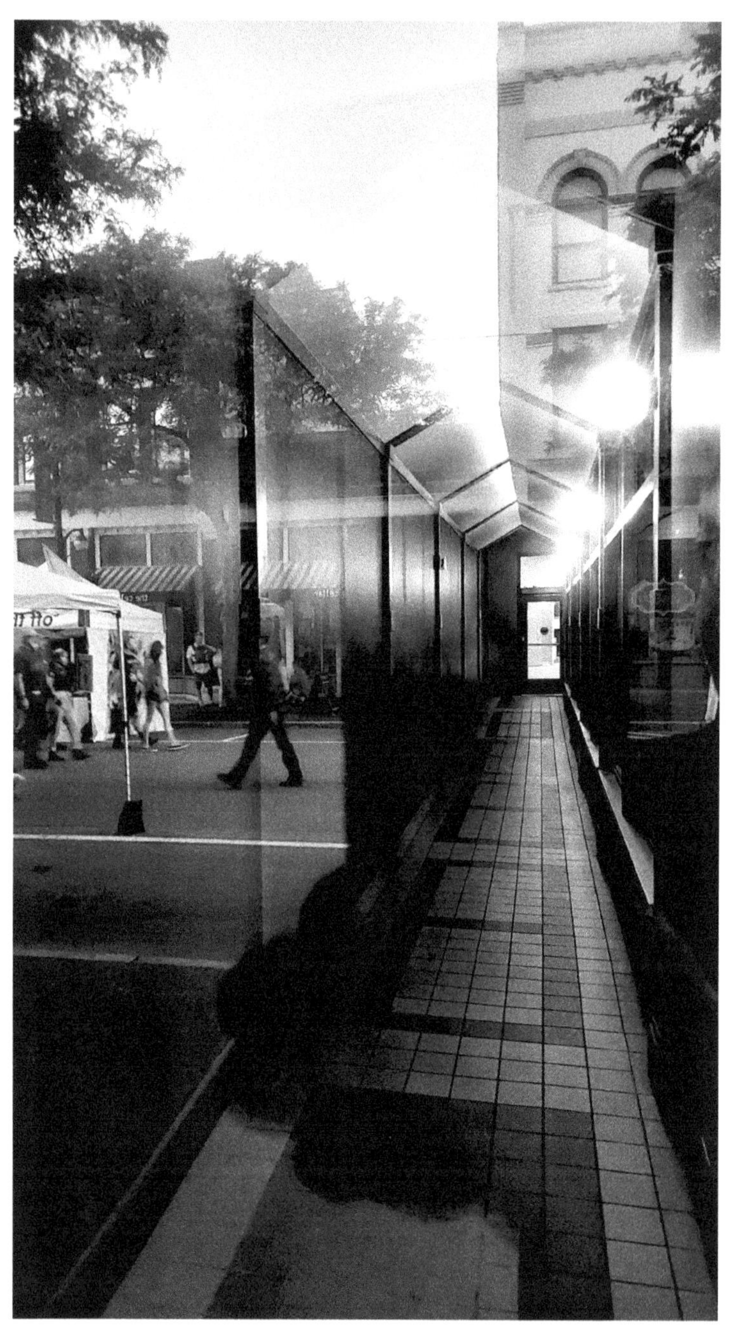

Cloister

Though I have taken vows, though I walk this path black-robed, hands folded, I am not blind. I see the young woman in shorts, the jaunty-jeaned man I might have been, the tent set for whatever feast day this fellowship celebrates. Whatever profane thing in which I must not, can not, participate. You may say it is my own choice, my cynical hermeticism, which seals me off from the laity, the flock, the world. And on certain days I agree. On those days I walk elsewhere than here, a different corridor, a sanctum sanctorum with only one view, and that not outward. But this corridor—this cloister of guilty pleasure—I have built with my own hands, blessed with my own benediction, sacrilegious as it may be to the Brothers who never promenade here. I am tempted—tempted, I say—to pause, to genuflect, as if the Sacrament were exposed, though what I see beyond the glass is surely sin, error, the fall, even if of my own making, of my own self. The panes rattle, a devil's tongue of voices—Miles Davis, George Strait, Taylor Swift, calling from the tent. I press my hand to the trembling glass. Covet the exit at the distal end. Later, in my cell, I will remove the scapula, apply the lash. God help me.

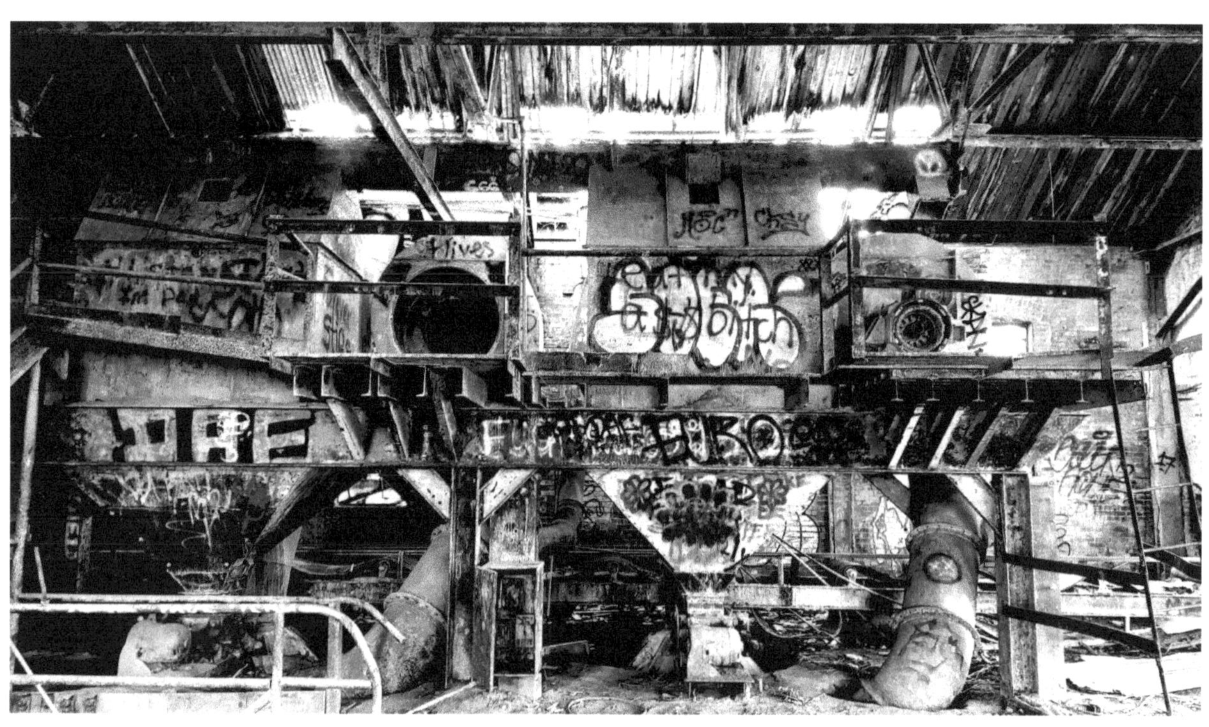

Judgement Day

through cement
earth
whatever lies beneath

up thrust arms
hungry
unloved
looking for
an embrace

ravaging refuse of
paradise
they seek to drag down
souls
angels
gods

play dead
they will know
someone is here
they feel

thought moving
breath breathing
hearts beating

bracelets of macho

tattoos in unknown languages
black-hearted Samson arms

pull down temple pillars
our handiwork
scrawled across
rusted lintels of Eden

sweat of the brow
rust

thorn and thistle
brush

dust
has come to claim us

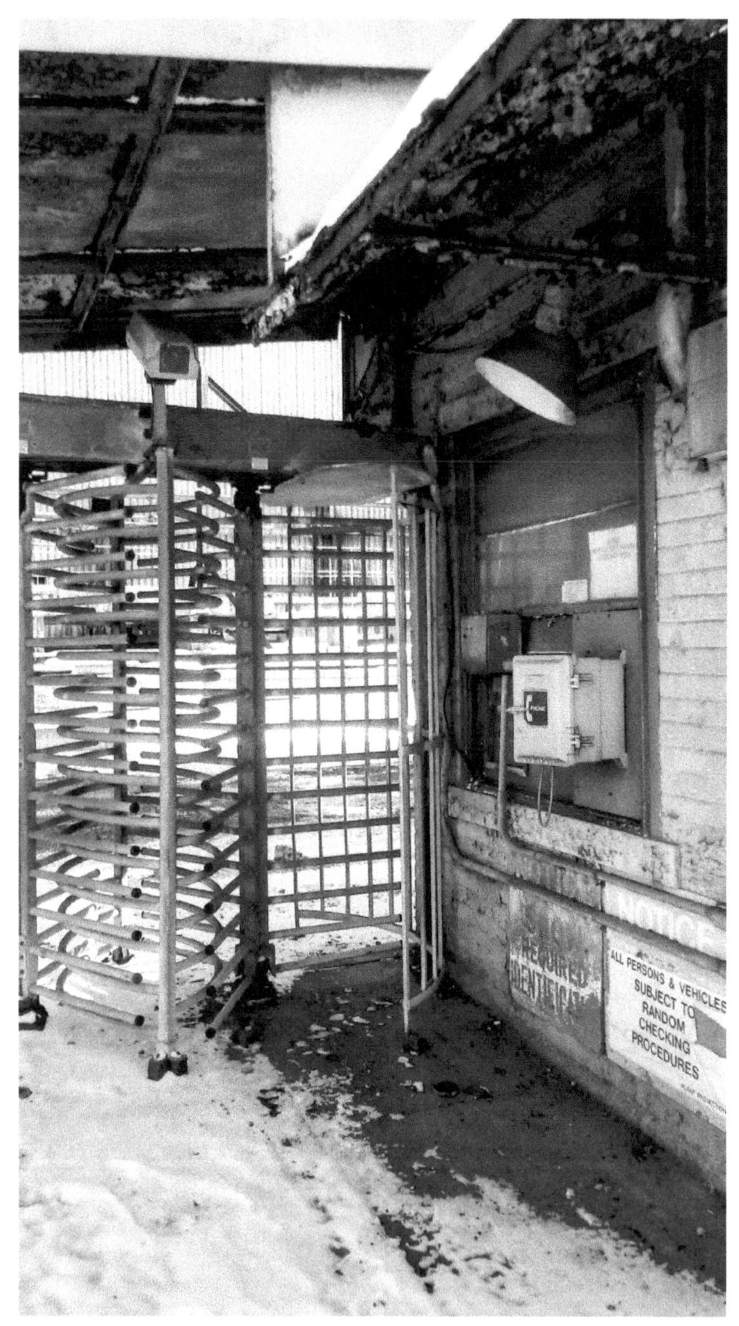

REQUIRED
IDENTIFICAT
NOTICE
ALL PERSONS & VEHICLES
SUBJECT TO
RANDOM
CHECKING
PROCEDURES

Subject To

Yes, it's a cold day in hell here
at Random Checking. We probe

everywhere: groin, spleen, thyroid—
what's inside that left eyeball?

Never mind, we'll find it.
Body cavity? We don't search 'em,

we make 'em. We prefer a running
start. You want out, we want in.

What'd you have for breakfast...
yesterday? We want to know.

We keep spread sheets, actuarial tables,
risk-neutral measures. We report

to everybody. We use Linotype, teletype,
genotype, stereotype. And, for a nominal fee,

we'll archetype. Perhaps you misunderstood
the sign. We don't check randomly; we check

for randomicity. Think your event horizon
is undetectable? Think again, Einstein. Nothing

escapes our probing metal fingers. Oh, and your
ID? We already have it. Pondering that

call box now, eh? The one labeled "Phone?"
Go ahead. Try and open it. It might work.

Might not.

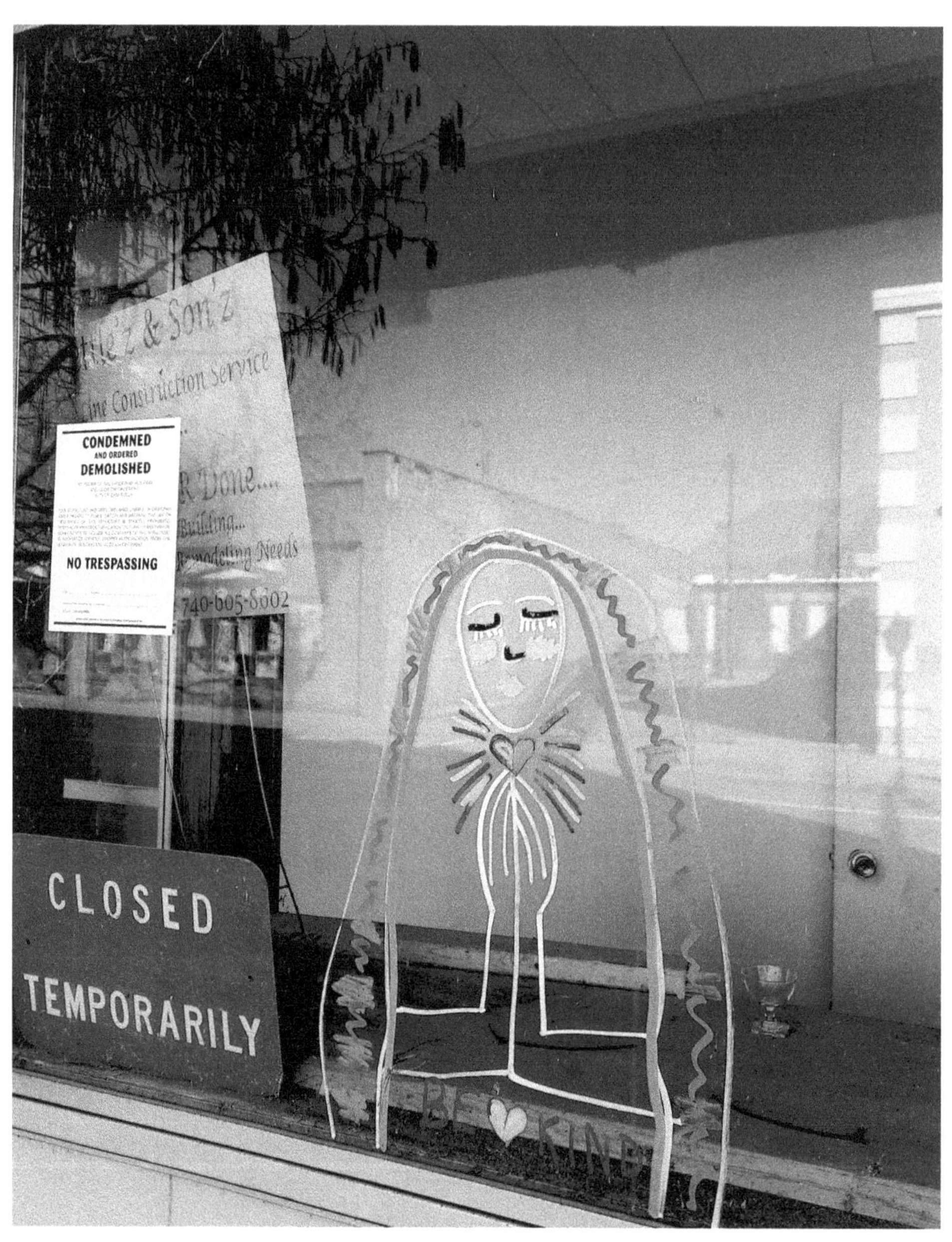
...tie'z & Son'z
...ine Construction Service
CONDEMNED
AND ORDERED
DEMOLISHED
NO TRESPASSING
...R Done...
...Building...
...Remodeling Needs
740-605-8002
CLOSED
TEMPORARILY

Temporarily Condemed

Please pardon our inconvenience.
Our world, it seems, has gone to hell.

We have reached out to Dante,
but Virgil is missing and Beatrice

has turned a cold shoulder. We would
offer up the Grail Cup behind us, but

you cannot come in to collect, and we
are condemned to adhere to the rules,

or, more specifically, this window pane,
though we are happy here as you can see

from our prayerful aspect and lustrous long
lashes. With a blush, we offer our hearts, our

full lips, and a phone number you can call
should you have any remodeling needs, though

so far it has not done us much good. We hope for
better connection in the next incarnation. We hope

for a better world to come. We hope you will be kind.
Namaste. Welcome. The sky is falling. We hope.

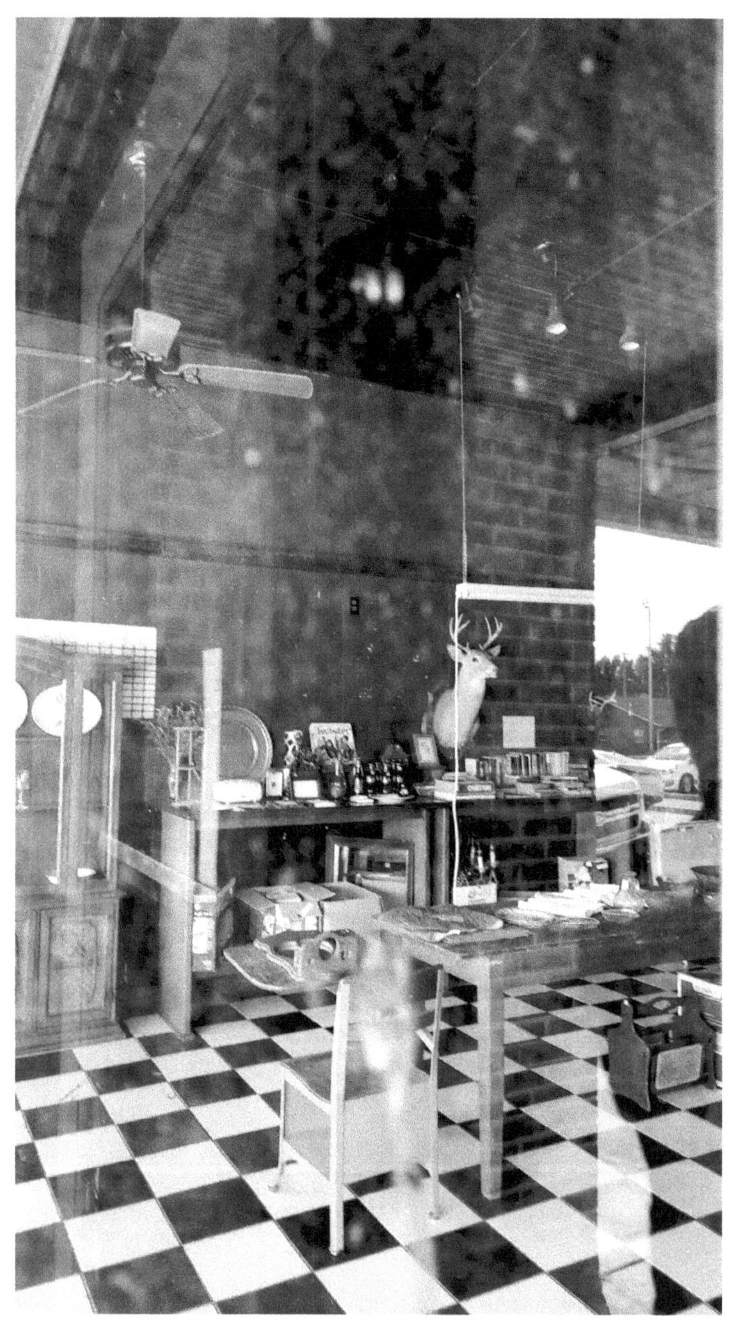

Twister

We blew through, no walls or windows shattered,
only this wake, these things, and a freight-train rumbling
which has passed with the night. Beer bottles, Chilton,

mine. China cabinet, yours. China, what is left of it,
silver goblet, though we both drank from it, yours.
Place settings, the table upon which they set, we

shared that a while, though the careful wrapping
of the napkins is you. As is the mirrored candle-
holder flat on the writing desk, though once it hung

in a living room and once, if memory serves, I
gifted you it. And the desk? Both of us, facing,
in the beginning, a blackboard scribbled with

intimate equations. Solved, in the end, for zero.
Field and Stream, Better Homes and Gardens,
ghosts now, haunting the magazine basket

too often ignored. That photo behind the Chilton:
you, as I first saw you, perhaps in real time, perhaps
in the frame of memory. The books, both standing

and splayed, a library of what came after. The rest,
more difficult to divvy up. Flowers: dried now,
thorny then, vase of origin unknown. Serving plate,

display purposes only. A Harlequin tube of shifting sands
which dazzled us from time to time. Boxed reflections
of empty hopes and unwrapped dreams. Instruments

of torture, the hooks we sank into each other. Santa
parting the tableware, or is it a hula dancer with
coconut breasts? And, of course, our favorite game,

twisting, twining, plotting to upset, never a true
embrace. But, for the life of me, I can't quite place
the elk head. Something we immured, perhaps, Poe-like,

when we mortared that brick wall. Talisman? Fetish?
Beating heart? The future, as we envisioned it.
The happily ever after. If so, who gets it now?

Who wants it, now?

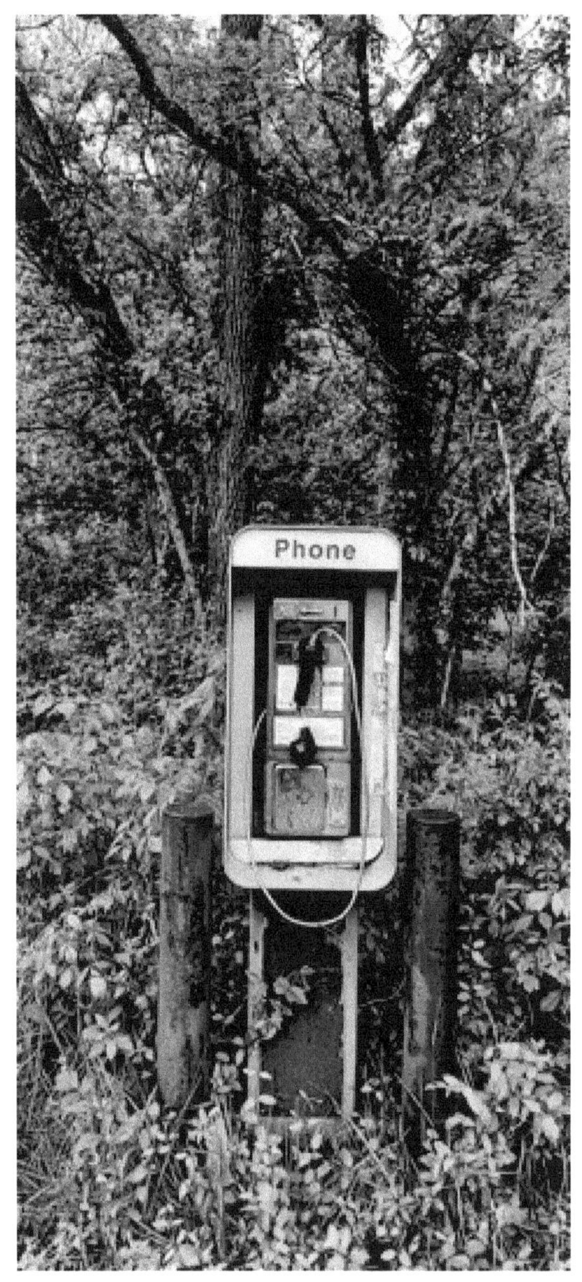
Phone

The Hang Up

They hear it in Ohio, Pennsylvania,
the cotton fields of the Llano Estacado,
the gator lands of south Florida,
the bottom of Crater Lake. Tsunami
warnings siren across the Pacific. Three mountains
in the Hindu Kush implode. Blood stains

your connection to civilization. You didn't know
Bakelite could cut so deep. It's 1983
and she's told you don't call her again,
no matter if you're lost in the woods in Hicksville,
or wherever, falling off a cliff. Sinking in quicksand,
goodbye, good riddance, good God.
Hasn't she had enough. Haven't you.

And here you are, four decades, three divorces,
two heart attacks, six grandkids later,
a middle of nowhere return, sanity hanging
by a thread, you wish you could pick it up,
put it back together, punch the right numbers,
say I'm sorry, wondering, isn't life funny, how you found
it again, how this thing is still here, your anger, your

hang up, if only you'd known. Leaves rustle. Wind blusters
in the open window. You start the car, head for the Interstate,
that lunatic asylum you saw in Weston. Shuttered now,
tourists and ghost hunters only, poems of the lost
tattooed on therapy room walls. You happen to have
a crayon on you. In the rear view, the phone rings.

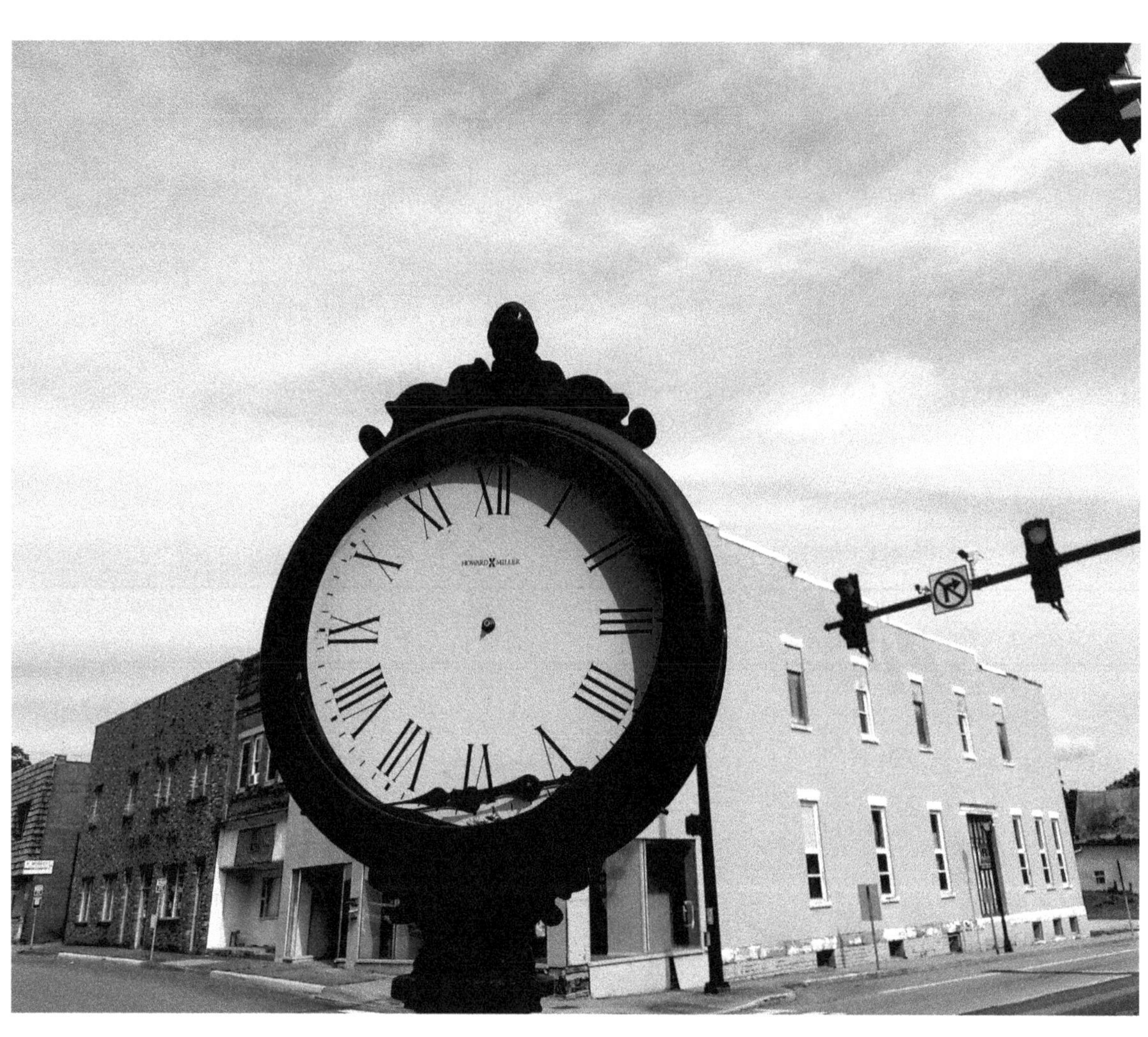

Standard Time

Is this how the world ends?
One screw loose, and it all falls

apart. Every thing we know, everything
we love, everything we are, screeches to a halt.

Empty streets
straight out of the Twilight Zone.

Traffic lights stuck on red. What's the point
of a no-right-turn sign

if we never make it to the intersection?
On the other hand, pun intended,

go left, young man.
This crossroads has got an angle,

but the march of time is at
parade rest, and we can't see it.

Wasps, or the spawn of some devil
prairie weed, lie feet up

beneath the even keel of eternity.
Question is, when did we join them?

The empty store front
sells no answers.

The sky threatens,
but will never carry through.

We, however, have no time on our hands,
and we are coming for you,

HowardXMiller.

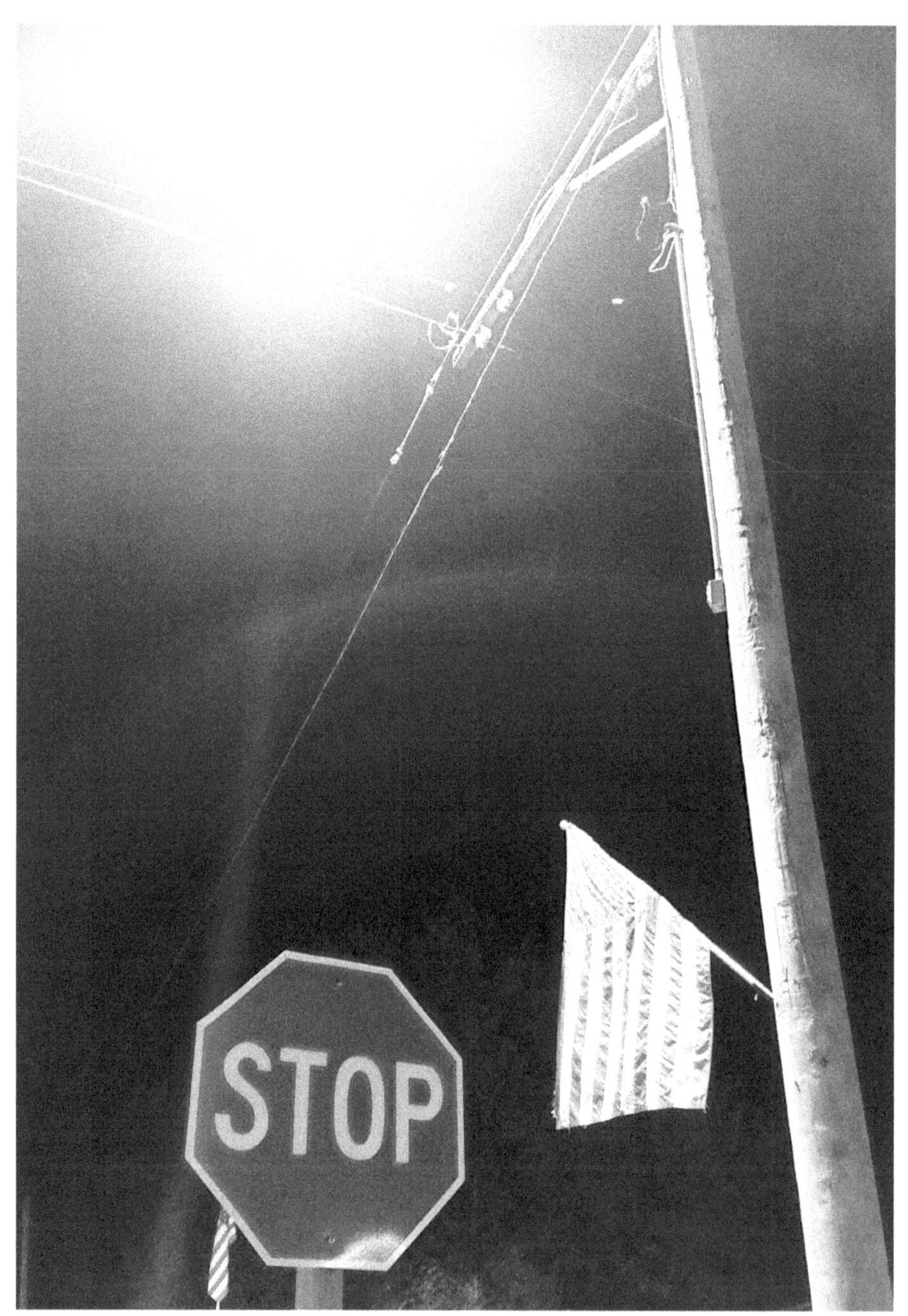

STOP

Stop

I drop into neutral and race the engine
and think of you and that flag you threw
and how I said What Where When

while you counted off the yardage
and I threw a challenge to no avail
no points scored

which was always a loss for me
right down to the wire
was always someplace over our heads

we never learned or we learned
too well and I could go on
with the football play-by-play

but it was never a game really
as I sit here deciding whether to
trip ahead wheel right maybe left

does it matter I don't think so
till I see that blur-in-the-dark rainbow
overarching STOP and I think

turn around go back yield the field
you didn't blow the whistle
the ball is still in play

I was wrong Baby O I was wrong
whatever it was
though that Hail-Mary pass could just be

the streak of my windshield wiper
and I can't seem to get myself
up off the gridiron

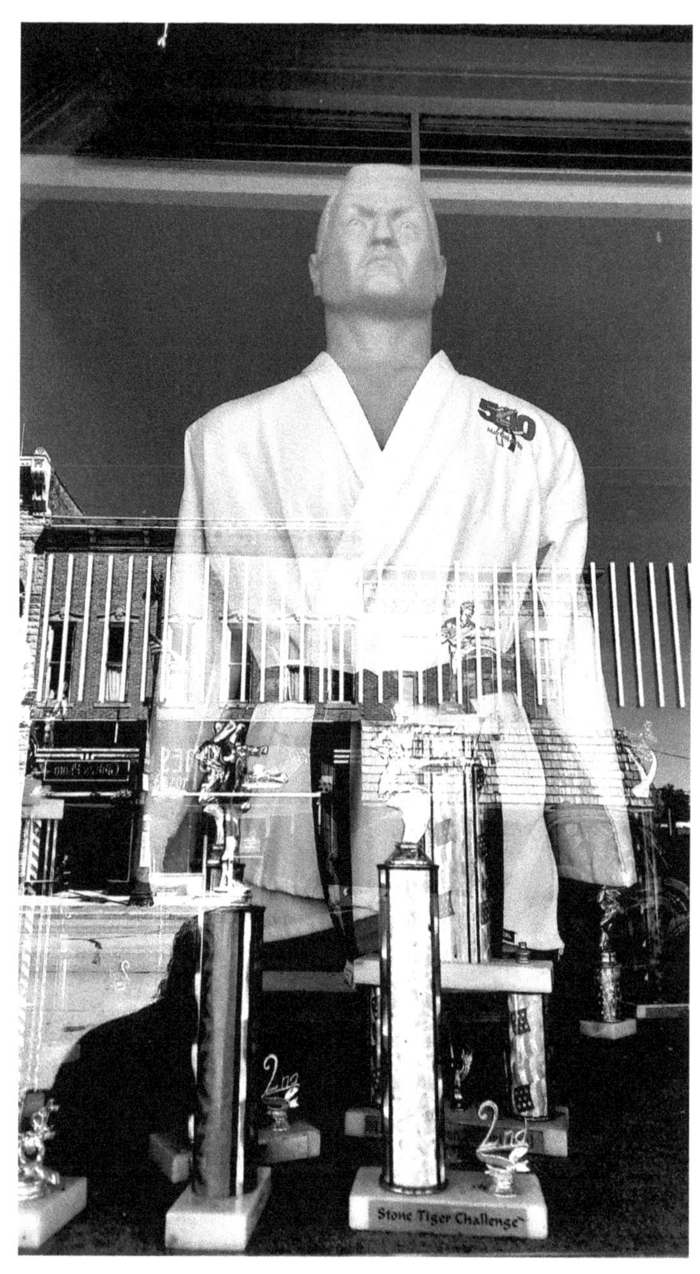

Stone Tiger Challenge

Window Dressing

He may be 2nd place
but he's rough, tough,
and black-belted,

a Stone Tiger Challenger,
not afraid to let us know

he can bad-ass bare foot
break our jaw, knock us

senseless with his titanium
cranium, his studied mix

of testosterone and Zen,
not just another pretty face.

Guardian of our Main Street,
like it or not, he greets
stranger and neighbor

with the same down-turned
horseshoe charm, marbleized
stare overlooking everything,

everyone, broad boxed shoulders
trying to shrug our attention
away from the fact

he's only half a man
with no grip on reality

and nothing hanging out
his sleeves to grip it with.

Do we let him be? Do we
point out these certain flaws,

disturb his pride of second place
in the martial art of non-being?

Haven't we been here ourselves,
in this window, on display
on our worst days, our best,
those random moments

when the shit is flying
and kicks and head butts
yield no advantage?

Haven't we too
pulled the Stone Tiger's tail?
And come out 2nd?

We pass on by
and trust that he,
or some dummied-up
mannequin manifestation of us,

will be here always,
watching over

the ungraspable, unknowable parts
of ourselves, fending off
third and fourth place wannabes.

Especially on a day
like today, so deceptively
calm and shitless.

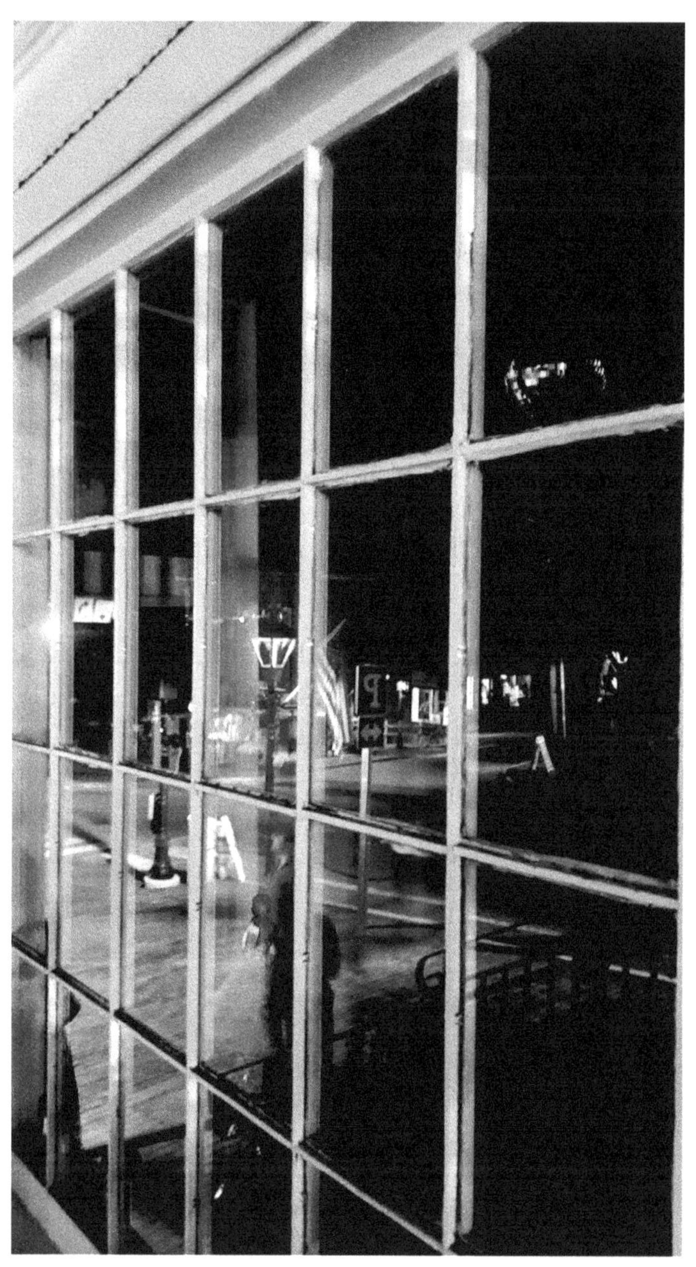

The Night Window

That face. You grope for a name—is that a beard? A hat? A white stick? Could he be blind, staring straight ahead like that? Do you know a blind man? You did once, maybe—Sunday School, Homer, Milton, Beckett, the knife thrower at the carnival when you were ten—but the feet are wrong, all out of whack, they don't line up with the torso, they don't face forward, they are coming your direction. You know them, those pointed, shiny black boots. Or should. What are they doing on your street? If this is, indeed, your street. The banister, the ornate iron which the man is passing, it's not yours, it doesn't lead to your house—at least, not this house, here, tonight.

You push up on the wood rails. The window doesn't give. Nothing gives. No egress, no chance of communication. Only disconnection. You will never speak to this man. Never truly see him. And yet, he is always here. Always in passing. You can hear his stick tap. Night after night. Tapping. Cradling that doll.

Your childhood. That's your childhood in his arms. Now you know where it went. It never left. It's right outside. You can't touch it, but it's there. You'll never get it back, he'll never let it go, look at the way he clings to it, that man. He took it the night you abandoned your parents' roof. The night you first penetrated a lover. The night you realized the dark was real, and you were destined for it. This night you realize he will always be out there, him and the babe in arms, passing by on this street—the street where you are—with pieces of a life dismembered, a life misplaced, a life, sometimes, you hope, well-lived. A life, certainly, well-haunted.

And, though tomorrow night it will flame out, an echo—his name, their name, your mother's voice, calling, like the light on the pole you thought you had lost track of—fires your subconscious.

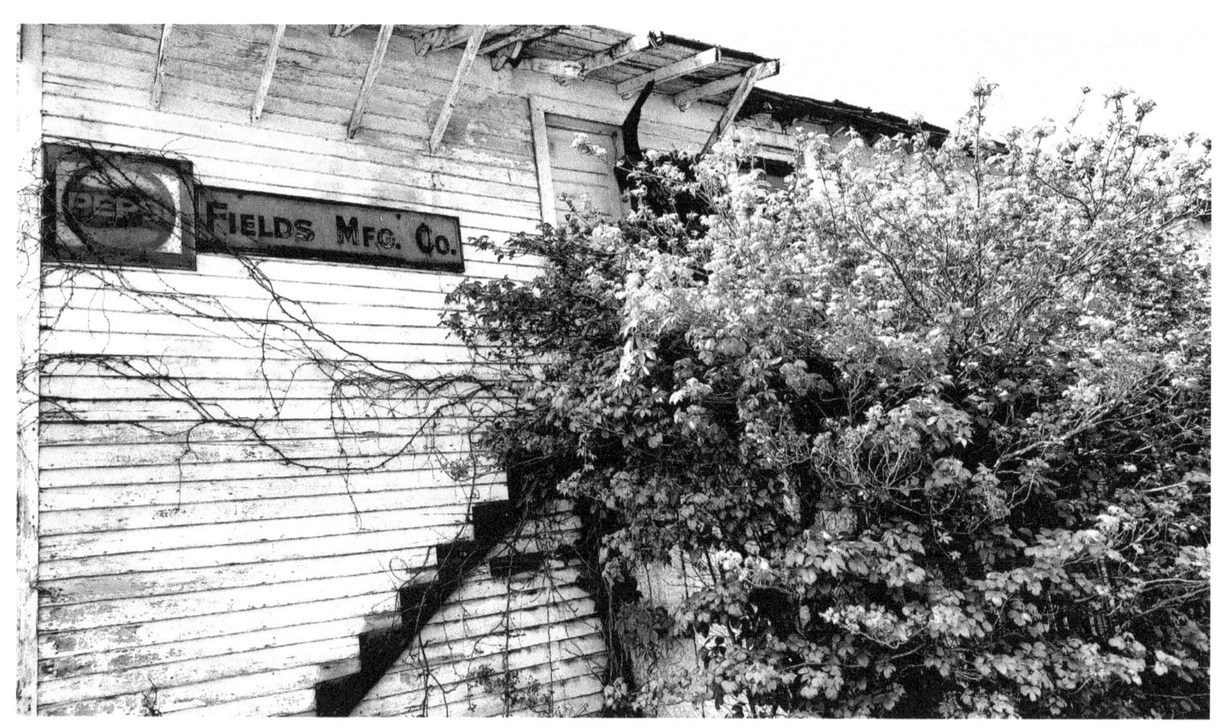
PEPSI
FIELDS MFG. CO.

A Blossom Fell

somewhere
lights are low
cigarettes ghost
King Cole croons

one of us still clings
long boney fingers
love-knotted joints
the other unmoved

which of us is which
is the dream of a lyric
read on the face
of the other
the morning after

that slow dance
remember
we barely moved
body against body
ravenous thrusts
moonbeams drifting
your place or mine

how different
the day looks
paint peeling
windows shuttered
thorns exposed

unnatural
for such as us
to say

I love you

yet

one caresses
one doesn't move
how dare it continue

impossible
embrace

somewhere
lights low
cigarette ghosts
blossoms fall

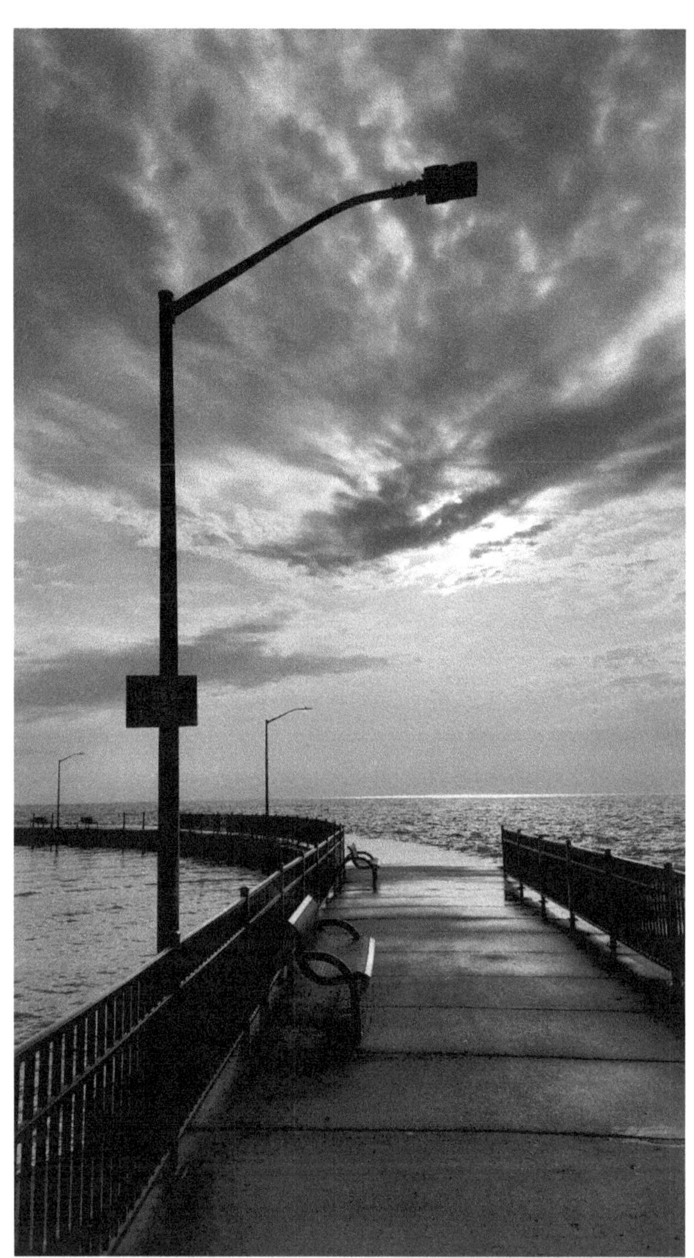

Luna Pier

Absence. That is what is here, the absent.
Fishermen, tourists, cloud-gazers, motor

boats, the wind, all absent. And now
I add you to the scene. Squarely within frame,

next the laugh-mouthed children. Though,
can I miss what I never had? Possession

is nine-tenths of the law. I had the other tenth.
I had a ghost, a dream, a few words strung

like cloud-bellies in air. Love, life.
But neither of us consulted a dictionary.

That glow, that lost horizon thermonuclear
remnant of some foreign, absent, ravaged land. What if

I dive in, stroke for it—the butterfly, no,
the breast? Can I reach it before the sun flees

refuge? Before Christ returns and pulls forth
fishes and loaves? Can I swim with a miracle

in my pocket? For you were, you know, I say
to no one, my miracle. False prophet that I am,

I had predicted sun in someone's hair.
Someone's hand in someone's hand.

I sit, pull my jacket tighter.
Absence. Chill caress upon the heart.

Location names of photos paired with texts:

Breath of the Lord: Roadside, New York, pg. 1
Heaven From Here: Hinton, West Virginia, pg. 5
Airstream: Mexicantown, Detroit, pg. 7
Modern, and Other -isms: North Side Pittsburgh, Pennsylvania, pg. 11
Smile You Are: Bellevue, Ohio, pg. 13
Old Style: Blue Mound, Illinois, pg. 15
Home Town Girl: Chambersburg, Pennsylvania, pg. 17
Cat People: Clinton, Illinois, pg. 19
BOLO: Morrisonville, Illinois, pg.21
Dead Man's Hollow: Dead man's Hollow Conservation Area,
    Pennsylvania, pg. 23
Look Up: Black Lick, Pennsylvania, pg. 27
A Well-Lighted Place: Ladonnia, Missouri, pg. 31
Escape: Lorain, Ohio, pg. 33
Full Immersion: Fredonia, New York, pg. 35
Cloister: Corning, New York, pg. 37
Judgement Day: Black Lick, Pennsylvania, pg. 39
Subject To: Weirton, West Virginia, pg. 43
Temporarily Condemed: Zanesville, Ohio, pg. 45
Twister: Belle, Missouri, pg. 47
The Hang Up: Walkersville, West Virginia, pg. 51
Standard Time: Point Pleasant, West Virginia, pg. 53
Stop: Belle, Missouri, pg. 55
Window Dressing: Van Wert, Ohio, pg. 57
The Night Window: Wicasset, Maine, pg. 61
A Blossom Fell: Mouth of Wilson, Virginia, pg. 63
Luna Pier: Luna Pier, Michigan, pg. 67

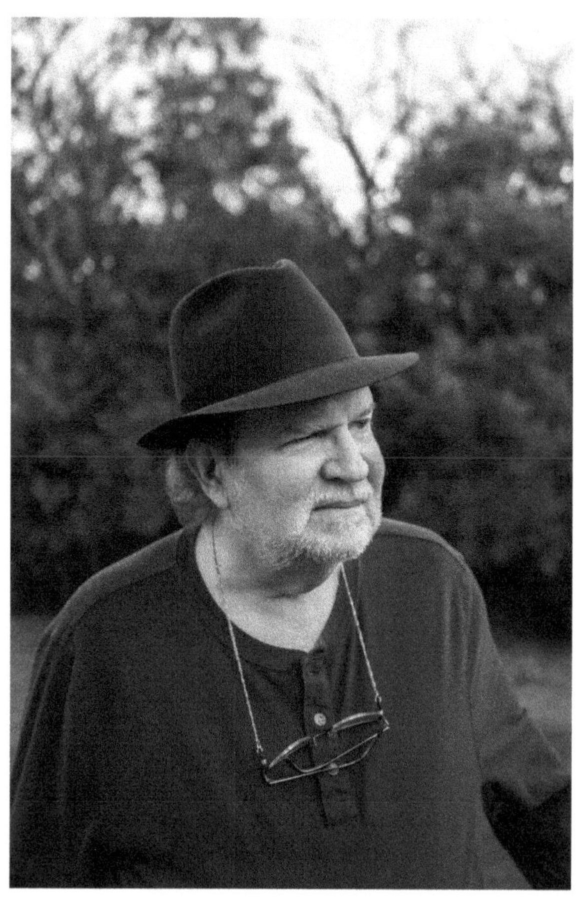

Robert L. Dean, Jr. is the author of *Pulp* (Finishing Line Press, 2022), *The Aerialist Will not be Performing: ekphrastic poems and short fictions to the art of Steven Schroeder* (Turning Plow Press, 2020), and *At the Lake with Heisenberg* (Spartan Press, 2018). A multiple Best of the Net and Pushcart nominee, his work has appeared in many journals and reviews. A native Kansan, Dean has been a professional musician and worked at *The Dallas Morning News*. He lives in Augusta, Kansas, along with a universe of books, CDs, LPs, and a couple dozen hats. He enjoys chess and backgammon, when he can find someone willing to play.

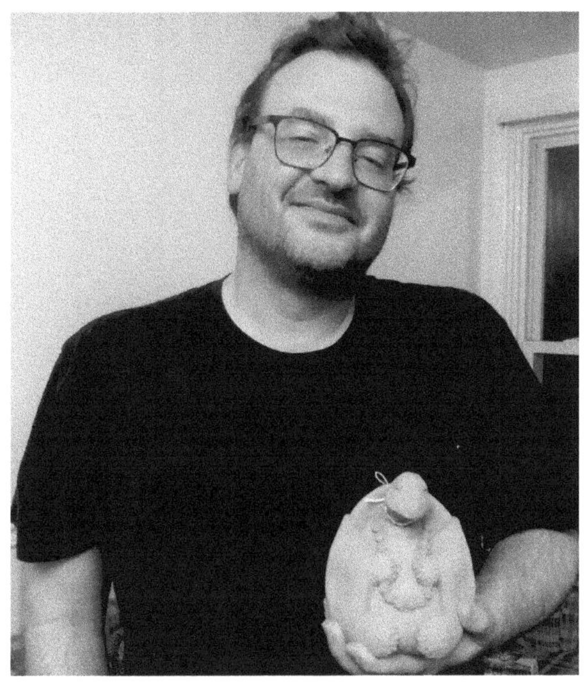

Jason Baldinger is a poet and photographer from Pittsburgh, PA. He is the co-editor of *Trailer Park Quarterly* and co-runs The Odd-Month Reading Series. He's penned twenty books of poetry the newest of which include; *American Aorta* (OAC Books) *Waiting on Hummingbirds* with Kansas poet James Benger (Their fourth together) His first book of photography, *Lazarus* (OAC Books), was released last year and the ekphrastic collaboration *Hope is a Prison* with poet Rebecca Schumejda (OAC Books) was just released. More ekphrastic collaborations are in the works featuring his photography in 2025. His poems and photos have appeared across a wide variety of online sites and print journals. You can hear him read from various books on Bandcamp and on lps by The Gotobeds and Theremonster.

This project was made possible, in part, by generous support from the Osage Arts Community.

Osage Arts Community provides temporary time, space and support for the creation of new artistic works in a retreat format, serving creative people of all kinds — visual artists, composers, poets, fiction and nonfiction writers. Located on a 152-acre farm in an isolated rural mountainside setting in Central Missouri and bordered by ¾ of a mile of the Gasconade River, OAC provides residencies to those working alone, as well as welcoming collaborative teams, offering living space and workspace in a country environment to emerging and mid-career artists. For more information, visit us at www.osageac.org

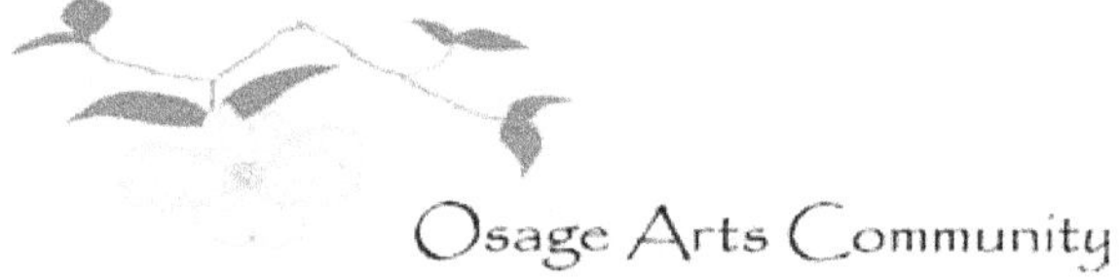